THE MAJOR LOOKS OVER HIS SHOULDER

THE MAJOR LOOKS OVER HIS SHOULDER

A Medical Memoir of World War II

by

MAJOR VINCENT P. MARRAN
United States Army Reserve, Retired

MANOR HOUSE PUBLISHING

MANOR HOUSE PUBLISHING
615 Coddingtown Center, Suite 187
Santa Rosa, CA 95401

Copyright © 1989 Vincent P. Marran, D.M.D., B.S.
All rights reserved.

No part of this book may be reproduced or transmitted in any form or by any means electronic or mechanical, including photocopying, recording, or by any information storage and retrieval system, without the written permission of the copyright owner, except for brief quotations embodied in reviews.

Library of Congress Cataloging in Publication Data

Marran, Vincent P., 1915-
   The major looks over his shoulder : a medical memoir of World War II / by Vincent P. Marran.
   p. cm.
   ISBN 0-942383-08-7 : $11.95
   1. Marran, Vincent P., 1915- . 2. World War, 1939-1945—Medical care—United States. 3. World War, 1939-1945—Medical care—Europe. 4. World War, 1939-1945—Campaigns—Western. 5. World War, 1939-1945—Personal narratives, American. 6. Soldiers—United States—Biography. 7. Oral surgeons—United States—Biography.
I. Title.
D807.U6M37 1989
940.54'7573'092—dc20
[B]   89-12746
                                                                        CIP

To Kitty, who first conceived this book after hearing me relate several episodes of my part in World War II. Her love and encouragement bore the fruit of what follows along with a deep emotional look into this part of my personal past.

CONTENTS

DEDICATION ix
1. OUTWARD BOUND — ENGLAND 1
2. GENERAL PATTON'S THIRD ARMY.... 7
3. NORMANDY — JUNE 1944 19
4. ROAD CONVOY 39
5. FROM GI'S TO GENERAL 57
6. DIVISION CASUALTY
   CLEARING STATIONS 65
7. METZ 77
8. THE ROAD TO THE BULGE 83
9. THE SAAR 93
10. OPERATIONAL POLICIES 99
11. PRUM AND THE SIEGFRIED LINE 105
12. THE RHINE 113
13. STARVATION CAMP 125
14. APOLDA 139
15. BUCHENWALD 153
16. CZECHOSLOVAKIA 159
17. THE RUSSIANS ARRIVE 165
18. SALZBURG 175
19. BERCHTESGADEN 181
20. HOMEWARD BOUND 189
    EPILOGUE 193

DEDICATION

During World War II it was my privilege to wear the shoulder patch of General George S. Patton's 3rd Army. I was honored to serve with the enlisted medics of that great outfit.

You won't see them in the old newsreels of marching infantry or clanking armor. Yet they were there; when and where it counted.

On the firing line the aidman hugged the ground with his medical kit. The crack of M1 rifles echoed in his ears along with the bark of common company's howitzers lobbing 105mm shells overhead.

He left the questionable shelter of his armored halftrack emblazoned with red crosses to race with a buddy to a disabled smoking tank. There, usually under fire from the enemy, they evacuated the wounded crew.

Back in the aid station he held one hand high with a unit of blood plasma while his other hand felt for a pulse. Murmured prayers that the GI on the litter would come out of shock escaped his lips. A few feet away a buddy checked for bleeding as he changed a dressing.

The ambulance driver helped load wounded passengers and wondered again how he could make a road fit only for a demolition derby seem like brand new hardtop.

At the field or evacuation hospital strong arms gently took the loaded litters from the ambulance. They steadied them while a medical officer quickly checked the nature of the wounds and directed litter bearers.

He stood calmly and competently across from the surgeon in the surgical tent. To quiet commands he sponged the wound, passed instruments, and prepared sutures and dressings. Two years ago he was selling hardware.

In the ward tent he made his rounds with compassion and concern. Florence Nightingale, after her gender shock, would have approved. A little over two years ago he was a bricklayer.

This book therefore, is dedicated to those heroes without guns. They served so well both their country and their God.

Chapter 1

OUTWARD BOUND — ENGLAND

I hit the brakes suddenly for the second time in fifteen minutes damning the blackout conditions which masked intersections and route numbers. My highway navigation wasn't helped by the kaleidoscope of events whirling in my mind.

I was returning to Camp Miles Standish, an embarkation camp just south of Boston. Thanks to a magnanimous gesture by a friendly colonel there, and the loan of his car, I was able to make some last minute goodbyes. I only had time for a few minutes at Mercy Hospital in Springfield, Massachusetts saying goodbye to my wife and newly-born daughter.

In Holyoke, Mom had shed some tears. Dad squared his shoulders, stepped back a little, and in a voice choked by emotion said he wished he was going with me. He ended with a crisp, "Good luck, Major." My studied composure cracked as I started the car.

The kaleidoscope whirled on as I tried to remember highway turns and intersections on the dark roads.

I remembered that unforgettable radio announcement during the Chicago Bears football game. The announcer broke in with the fateful pronouncement; the Japanese had bombed Pearl Harbor. The United States was at war!

My Dad looked up and in his controlled voice suggested, "You'd better polish the buttons on your blouse." This proved prophetic. I was an Army Reserve Officer in the Dental Corps. Two weeks later I received an "Immediate Action" telegram for a physical examination preliminary to orders for active duty.

This was but one of many reminiscences bouncing around in my mind as I drove. There was the tour of duty at Fort Adams in Newport, Rhode Island where I had performed a lot of oral surgery. The ninety-day crash course in maxillo-facial surgery at Harvard Medical School, and Massachusetts General Hospital where we were bombarded with information. The memorable months as oral surgeon at Fort Devens Station Hospital. Our first child, a daughter Ann, was born there. Memories abounded.

The spinning images stopped abruptly. I hit the brakes as a uniformed figure with arm upraised was silhouetted in my high beams. I stopped. "Get in corporal, where away?" I greeted him. He spotted the officer's uniform and hesitated. "Come on in, it's just another GI," I said. He got in. "Miles Standish?" I suggested. He nodded. Two intimate strangers sharing an underlying anxiety about the future. There was an immediate bond. We small talked the rest of the way. We both needed it.

The posting to the Fourth Auxiliary Surgical Group outside of Atlanta, Georgia pleased me. I needed the training, I knew I was headed overseas eventually. The training passed too quickly. Eventually was here.

Dawn came rapidly. A hand rocked my shoulder waking me. At breakfast we all ate with one eye open. A large manila envelope replaced the metal breakfast tray. "Orders for your detachment, Sir," a crisply attired sergeant said as he saluted. It turned out I was senior to over sixty medical and dental officers shipping out on one of the troop convoy's transports. The sergeant, after marching us to a long string of old railroad coaches stepped back and saluted smartly. "Good luck, Sir," he said. Somewhere down the line of cars a locomotive tooted as we boarded.

At a solemn twenty-five miles an hour, the train proceeded to the Boston army base docks. I boarded the waiting freighter, looked up at the bridge, then across the deck. About thirty feet away a genial-looking colonel with the suggestion of a smile on his face caught my eye. I walked over to him and we shook hands. He dismissed formalities with a grin and said that we'd get together a little later. We needed to assign some of our medical officers to staff the ship's infirmary.

It was then the full impact of what was happening hit me.

My memories drifted to a day early in 1938 at Harvard Dental School. I remembered the pitch of the Army and Navy recruiters for their respective dental corps. The Navy man stressed clean living, good meals, ship or shorebased clinics, and good equipment. Then there was the Army man, a realist to the core. "You will eventually be in the field," he started. He promised variations of discomfort from freezing cold to stifling heat, and sand, mud, and dirt for a floor. He added with a piercing look, "You'll have lousy rations, and no rations at times. It can be tough, but if you do your job, you will enjoy a respect and camaraderie that you will never experience again."

There was a stunned silence. I grinned. Having backpacked almost every peak in the White Mountains, I was accustomed to the outdoors and could read terrain maps and compass. Yes, I knew about the mud, sand and sweat. I could deal with it. I was his man. His description turned out to be absolutely right all the way.

Graduation was June 1938. I walked across Harvard Yard with several classmates, held up my right hand, and became a First Lieutenant in the Army Dental Corps Reserve. The memory was as fresh as yesterday. My kaleidoscope of memories kept spinning until sleep restrained it hours later.

I awoke at dawn in the crowded top deck cabin. We were at sea. There were six of us, five infantry captains and myself. Laboriously, I wriggled out of the bunk and shouldered open the unfamiliar door. I drew up sharply. Convoy! Ships and more ships ringed by destroyers and destroyer escorts. Smack in the center was a heavy cruiser and battleship. The scuttlebutt said the big Navy ships were the cruiser Augusta and the battleship Texas.

The ship's speaker blared the announcement that the first mess-sitting was coming. I headed below, acknowledging to myself that I was slightly woozy and hoping it would soon pass. About halfway through the slowly eaten breakfast there was a deep resounding thud. The messware jumped an inch off the tables. It sounded and felt like a giant hammer had hit the bottom of the ship. Seconds later, it hit again. There was a rush to get topside. Astern, in the distance, we saw the waterspout plumes of depth charges. U-Boats!

I was fascinated by a destroyer escort nearby on our port beam. She was rolling heavily in the swells toward the rear of the convoy and was barely under way. "Listen," suggested a navy crewman who appeared at my side. The detonations and waterspouts continued. Surprisingly, I forgot to be afraid. I was enthralled as we watched the escort vessels maneuver, constantly changing their protective screen as others tracked down the U-Boats. Later in the day we exulted when the ship's speaker announced a confirmed sub kill. By this time, I was in the ship's sick bay working out a duty roster. I wanted to ensure it was well-staffed by our medics.

Troop carriers crowded the harbor at Glasgow, Scotland. Furry-tongued retired generals were busy making the rounds welcoming the troops with, what they fondly hoped were inspirational speeches. The huge Queen Elizabeth in battleship grey, ghosted in at dusk carrying a full infantry division. She had left alone several days after us. Her high speed prevented escorts from keeping up with her.

From Glasgow we went to Evesham in the southern half of England. This was in market-garden country and about twelve miles from Stratford-on-Avon. Our group and other American personnel were billeted around the area, many with private families. I stayed with a market gardener and his wife who did their best to make me feel comfortable.

The group was not in limbo long about our assignment. We were Patton's, assigned to his new Third Army. There were mixed reactions among the men. No one was neutral. Opinions ranged from fearful, "Good God, he'll get us all killed," to realistic, "We'll sure see plenty of action," to optimistic, "Third Army will sure as hell help win this war."

I was in the latter group. I remembered a warm fall day in New York City in 1939. I was doing postdoctoral work at Columbia's School of Dental and Oral Surgery at the Medical Center. It was near the George Washington Bridge, so at lunchtime a few of us walked over to the bridge. We wanted to see "the one and only Armored Brigade of the U.S. Army" clank across the bridge into Manhattan.

Its commander had stumped long and loud for tanks and light armor. He was the flashy Colonel George S. Patton. "Even designs his own uniform," remarked Dr. Totten a former infantryman in World War I. With a portentous intuition he added, "We'll hear from this guy one of these days, he's got the right idea and knows what he's doing."

Chapter 2

GENERAL PATTON'S THIRD ARMY

It had been five years since I saw Patton's brigade on the bridge. Remembering that day, I sat there grinning as I sewed the Third Army shoulder patch on my left sleeve. I was now a member of the celebrated and controversial General George S. Patton's Third Army. Reporters of history have many stories to tell about the notorious Patton.

I never accepted the reporters' description of the slapping incident. In fact, I know for certain it had been greatly distorted. A few miles away from Evesham was the very field hospital where the incident occurred. It had been moved from Sicily to England.

As medics will do, we visited each other. A couple of us had talked with the medical officer and nurse who were there at the time of the incident. Their account indicated the whole story had not been told. What was not reported were the extenuating circumstances which triggered the general's reaction.

The incident happened in a ward tent of one of the evacuation hospitals. There were about two dozen GI's lying on cots with wounds of varying severity. The GI in question approached General Patton and began to cry out fearfully about the terrible war. The GI's tirade had an immediate effect on the wounded. They became quite agitated and some cried out.

General Patton, unable to calm the soldier, gave him a light slap on the face. Correspondents in Sicily agreed not to report this incident to their editors. They realized the possible ramifications. But one reporter broke the voluntary blackout for his own gain.

The witnesses story placed the incident in a different light. The provocation had been extreme. As the medical officer put it, "The general's reflexes were better than mine, my fist was well on its way when he beat me to it. Too bad, nobody would have tried to shake the earth over a mere captain."

I had a similar experience just west of the Rhine. It happened as I entered an abandoned old house serving as a casualty clearing station. An enlisted man with a gunshot wound of the upper left arm rose unsteadily to his feet. He began to scream obscenities hysterically punctuated with repetitions of, "we're all going to be killed." The other wounded soldiers were very upset by this and many demanded he "shut up!"

I tried calming him verbally. When that wasn't effective I lightly slapped his face. He immediately became silent and looked at me with surprise. I placed my hand on his shoulder and he sat down with a dazed expression.

Dropping to one knee I assured him he was not

going to die. I explained he was aggravating his buddies. Many of whom were more seriously wounded than himself. He said nothing, avoided my eyes, and stared at the floor until a medical officer came to help him.

This experience was not unique. It happened frequently in clearing stations and small field hospitals. Placed in their proper perspective these episodes should be termed "therapeutic slaps," not angry reactions.

Soon came Patton's famous speech to Third Army's medical-dental officers. The speech articulated the general's dedication to his profession and his concern for the troops he would lead. It was the conclusion which came through loud and clear. He said, "Gentlemen, we will make every effort to get our wounded to you, but if we can't, I expect you to go to them. If need be, you are expendable. I expect the Third Army to have the finest medical service in the entire U.S. Army." In retrospect, I believe the medical history of the war in Europe shows how well we responded.

My pre-professional education at a liberal arts college included a good bit of Shakespeare. In fact, my one and only Shakespearean role was playing Lady Macbeth, in the sleepwalking scene, in a classroom run-through. Honest. The Shakespeare Memorial Theatre at Stratford-on-Avon was only a few miles away. Even GI's who normally asked "Who?" when Shakespeare's name was mentioned flocked there to see the plays of the great bard. The plays changed frequently and were beautifully presented . Frankly, I loved it and saw all his major works. A few of them twice. In that tension-relieved atmosphere before the main assault on Festung Europa, GI's to whom Shakespeare would have remained an unfamiliar name became rabid fans.

Finally one day a laconic message came in. "The motor pool has three closed lab trucks on six-by-six chassis, pick up at your earliest convenience or sooner." These were the three untried dental lab trucks of which much was expected. Only three for the entire Third Army. They would be busy.

It only took about forty-eight hours back at our base for us to learn we had far from perfect units. It would tax our ingenuity and improvisation skill. As senior of the three officers concerned, I immediately set up a crash test schedule. I wanted to uncover as many bugs as possible while we, hopefully, could still do something about them.

Equipment poured in the next few days. We settled down to checking it as fast as we could. We thought the electric hot plates to process emergency splints and dentures were a good idea. However, the portable gasoline-driven generator had only a two-kilowatt output and was inadequate for that along with lights and other lab equipment. We had a lot of trouble with the hot plates themselves later, finally scrapping them as heating elements promptly burned out. No replacements were available. We finally scrapped them.

The trucks had been equipped with blackout curtains that were good and made night operations possible. We were to do a lot of that on the continent.

The units were immediately dispersed to do needed dental work and give us experience.

Late in May 1944, my unit was working at 20th Corps Headquarters ensconced on a hill outside

Marlborough, England. It overlooked a sizable and significantly long airfield. One of my friends, assistant to the corps surgeon, invited me to come with him late one afternoon to the base.

Bivouacked around the perimeter was the 101st Airborne Division. Once we passed through security, we went to the office of the division surgeon. Before long, we were off the end of a runway helping them check medical supplies. We watched the medics load several large British-made gliders marked with big red crosses. I couldn't help thinking, "How are they ever going to get these things into the air?"

A few days later, we were awakened sometime before dawn by the drone of numerous aircraft engines. "D-Day" had arrived. My room was in an English family's house at the foot of the hill. Throwing on a uniform, I hitched a ride up to corps headquarters. To use the term "awe-inspiring" would be a massive understatement for the dramatic scene at the huge base. Down two long runways and an adjacent new shorter runway, thundered the indomitable C-47's. Each one towed a big British Westland plywood and canvas glider of the 101st Airborne.

In a Cecil B. DeMille-like production to end all DeMille productions, the gliders were airborne before their tow planes. In rapid succession, others raced down the runways. Once airborne, they climbed slowly for altitude and flew in wide circles. A bunch of us stood rooted to the spot scarcely breathing until hundreds of C-47's and their tows were in the air. Then the huge spirals slowly unwound drawing a giant black band across the sky as they headed for the channel and distant France. An officer made the sign of the cross and several followed suit. No one spoke for minutes.

It was only a few days later. The shrill whistles and sound of locomotives caught my attention one afternoon as we worked. Down in the valley along came a railway engine and a long string of converted passenger cars. Each had large red crosses painted on them. Casualties from Normandy were being brought inland to waiting hospitals. It was only the first of many trains like that. How many on those trains, I wondered, had we watched take off on D-Day?

It wasn't long before a short verbal order sent the boys and me in haste to our group headquarters. We repacked and buttoned up the trucks for movement to Portsmouth and the channel. When I found out that emergency requisitions for repair and new equipment would be considered I headed for Third Army's big supply depot. I got permission from the Group CO, Colonel Kind, to plead our case.

We needed more powerful generators and I had a very strong point for my own case. Edwards, my technician-maintenance man had, deliberately I suspected, badly overloaded our generator so it reeked of burned insulation and was inoperable.

The only thing available, the supply major said tongue-in-cheek, was a big, bulky five kilowatt job. It took five or six guys to lift and was basically for ordinance outfits. He felt sure I wouldn't want it. "I'd love it, Sir," I answered, much to his consternation. Having stuck his neck out I wasn't about to let him off the hook. I went on to suggest we had two other lab trucks that could use similar generators. His astonished expression said, "Quit while you're ahead, buster." I did, but filed a written request and explanation. It was implemented later in France.

I didn't dare leave without the generator. I was afraid we'd never get it if I did. The big bulky five-kilowatt generator when ensconced on top of a jeep had a Laurel and Hardy touch. The driver and I nursed the top-heavy load back at ten to fifteen miles an hour. We arrived among astonished group members. "Where's the trailer?", someone immediately piped up. The major at the supply depot had raised his voice some when I mentioned it. "A trailer for it? You're insane." I left, fast.

It fit into the back of the truck with only inches to spare. We had to lift it into the truck and take it out to use it. But it had the power I needed so it was only a minor inconvenience as far as I was concerned. I felt my men and I were ready.

Our vehicles went to Portsmouth in a "drivers only" road convoy, while the rest of the personnel went by train. We changed trains at Reading with an hour-and-a-half wait in a delightful old station. For the duration it was sporting a Red Cross canteen. The most interesting part for me was the three formally dressed English gentlemen. I saw them standing at one end of the waiting room in front of an ornately carved fireplace with slowly-burning logs. They were expertly balancing dainty cups and saucers.

After a few minutes' wait in line I had just accepted a proffered cup of Red Cross coffee and a donut. I was talking with some of our enlisted men when one of these gentlemen caught the eye of myself and my CO. They beckoned, and we both went over to them.

They were MP's, Members of Parliament. They introduced themselves and we replied with name and rank. Their primary interest seemed to be that our officers mingled with the enlisted men. They chatted with them and simply took their place in line at the Red Cross stand regardless of rank.

The MP's shook their heads, marveling at this type of U.S. Army democracy. We acknowledged that in permanent installations and bases there were separate officer's mess facilities. Yet, we explained that this was standard for us in the field. These men apparently liked this approach and said that the British Army just didn't do this type of thing. Then we had an innocuous visit with a nice, neighborly discussion about our respective lifestyles in peacetime.

The low hills around Portsmouth were dotted with pre-embarkation camps. They were temporary pauses en route to Normandy. Just the bare necessities for a few days. They consisted of bunkhouses, cold water taps, and a hurriedly constructed mess. It fed troops in continuous relays from dawn to dusk.

During the second night, we were awakened by the staccato-like sound of a low-flying aircraft. From briefings, I recognized it as a German V-1 flying bomb. It was growing nearer. When its timer cut off the engine, it would dive unceremoniously into whatever was beneath. I held my breath. There was no antiaircraft fire.

The engine suddenly cut off, seemingly right overhead. Instinctively, I tried to make myself smaller. It was an agonizingly long twelve to fourteen seconds. There was a loud roar not far away as the "buzz bomb" exploded on impact. The ground and flimsy bunkhouse shook violently. It had hit about a quarter of a mile away. Several people were killed and wounded, the grapevine declared at dawn.

The next morning, about 0900, the trucks rolled in to take us to the Portsmouth docks. Normandy was the next stop. D-day plus eight. The tight, closely intervaled trucks moved slowly out onto Portsmouth's streets.

Periodically, dozens of silvery grey barrage balloons hugged the ground in parks, playgrounds and cricket fields. The snouts of antiaircraft guns gazed skyward hungrily. Their skeleton crews relaxed in nearby shadows. A sprinkling of women, young children, and babies gazed fascinated from roadsides. The wild-eyed kids wore soiled, unkempt clothes. Their charmingly dirty faces were smeared with food and jelly.

Tall iron fences festooned with barbed wire in places, dispelled any idyllic thoughts. Formal gates and expedient gaps were reduced to billboard status by an alphabet soup of apparently meaningless small signs. Signs that obviously meant a lot to the right people.

The dock area swarmed with uniforms. An ordered chaos. Gangplank guardians gripping clipboards checked and double-checked each name before waving people aboard. The seemingly endless chain of uniforms snaked aboard a mini-fleet of small freighters, cross-channel steamers, and excursion boats. Our small cross-channel craft showed signs of more halcyon days. After head count checks, the pulse of the ship's engines nudged us clear of the dock. We moved slowly down the harbor to rendezvous with other troop carriers, supply vessels, and escorts.

There was a very light fog on the channel and the convoy formed up off the Isle of Wight. The escort vessels were never still and even with the light fog you could recognize an inner and outer line of protection.

As early dusk approached, the shifting escorts faded away. The upper structures of an armada of sunken ships, sacrificed to produce harbor-like conditions, heralded the low shores of Normandy.

Large numbers of chunky LCI's and a shipyard's menu of small craft wheeled and darted to ships' sides. A few bulky, more ponderous LST's drifted to shore to disgorge heavy equipment and troops.

Somewhere aboard our boat a very British-sounding bullhorn blasted, "Fourth Auxiliary Group, form up starboard amidships." "Shhh you dope, they'll hear you!", was my first reaction. Then I chuckled aloud. "They" had known we were there for a number of days.

An LCI (Landing Craft Infantry) isn't a big craft; hardly a boat. It is purely functional. Yet, in my wildest imagination, I would not have believed you could get that many men into the square footage. The boarding nets on the steamers' sides resembled a descending migration of giant spiders with GI's packs, rifles. There were arms and legs everywhere.

The bull-like voice on the bullhorn bellowed down to us on the LST. "Everybody there okay?" From the packed masses of GI's a high falsetto voice screamed, "No, where's Eleanor?" A roar of deep-throated laughter broke the pall of silence. The perfect tension-breaker.

In those troubled times, Eleanor Roosevelt ranged far and wide waving the flag and just being seen at home and overseas. It was no big deal at the time. It took a few years before the significance of this as a morale factor became appreciated.

We cast off and headed for the beach. It was dusk by now. Floating finger-like docks of steel pontoons made wet landings unnecessary at this point. A sergeant appeared out of the deepening dusk. He asked for unit identification and said we should follow him single file. Several hundred yards from the beach was a path bordered by lines of white tape. "Keep between the tapes," he cautioned, "land mines haven't all been cleared through here."

As dusk turned to dark we were lead to a hedgerow. There were a few trees, trampled vegetation, one sheet-steel stove of about twenty inches diameter and, lo and behold, some foxholes. Our bedrolls were "a couple of miles up the beach, somewhere."

Later, shadowy figures came along with "K" (field) rations which, at the time, were just about enough.

Chapter 3

NORMANDY — JUNE 1944

The foxholes were comforting along the stone wall and line of trees. The previous occupants had dug them well, for obvious reasons. The bonus was some dry hay in the bottom of each one.

Our bedding hadn't got to us and the early night air chilled more than we had expected. A few miles north of us the night sky suddenly erupted in a pyrotechnic display of antiaircraft fire. Apparently a few enemy aircraft had tried to sneak in, unsuccessfully.

The orders were, no smoking and no fires. As the evening wore on we paired off two to a foxhole and settled in head-to-toe. Sleep came grudgingly and dawn came fast. K-rations staved off hunger, barely. We needed the nourishment for the half-mile walk to waiting trucks. They took us to an assembly area where an evacuation hospital and a smaller field hospital were checking vehicles and supplies.

My truck, along with two other similar vehicles,

had arrived just before us. They had been offloaded onto a lighter to be brought ashore. The lighter had struck an underwater mine that the minesweepers had missed. Only heroic measures, like additional chains and counterbalancing with other movable cargo, had saved several vehicles from being dunked.

My men and I had packed our gear and supplies well so in a couple of hours we were ready to roll. Third Army was not yet operational. Some were farmed out on detached service to the Fourth Convalescent Hospital in the First Army area with another of the group's three dental units. The convalescent hospital was designated for soldiers able to return to duty fairly soon, such as those with minor wounds and illnesses like colds and flu.

There were two highlights in the several weeks tour of duty there. The first was a dramatic night air raid by German aircraft on our front lines using parachute flares to illuminate the target. Night skies over the combat line broke wide open with antiaircraft fire of all calibers, much of it tracer ammunition. You could read newsprint in the light, although we were several miles from the front lines.

Never to be forgotten was the huge sustained air strike by British and American bombers. They softened up enemy lines at Saint Lo for the Allied breakthrough. We lost count as squadron after squadron of four-engine bombers flew overhead. They etched a dark band of droning planes from England to the drop zone east of us, and westward back to bases in England.

Third Army plunged through the weakened German lines. Patton had unsheathed his saber.

Colonel Jim Weeks dropped by one day. The

colonel, a large heavily-built man with graying hair, was Chief of Dental Services, Third Army. I soon grew to love the genial guy. We talked operational policies, supplies and such. Then he grew quite serious and said, "We lost four men yesterday that should have made it." "What happened?" I responded. "During evacuation, one bled to death and three choked to death on their own blood and saliva." He stopped and looked at me intently.

"I'd say improper evacuation on their backs for the last three. Probably someone missed a bleeder and didn't tie it off on the first one."

"Bulls-eye," he nodded. "Any ideas?"

"Well, as a group," I replied, "we haven't had much experience with this sort of injury. So I suppose someone has got to get up to the casualty clearing stations and refresh memories on handling bleeders. They must be taught to understand that these cases have to be evacuated face down with a forehead strap to support the head. Then any saliva or oozing blood can drop out of the mouth."

He smiled and looking me right in the eyes, said, "Right, somebody's got to get up there and do just that." We talked a bit more about handling facial wounds. He broke off the discussion with, "Yeah, somebody's got to go up there." At the third, "somebody's got to go," I got the message and actually chuckled.

I nodded my head and said, "Okay Colonel, I'll go." Even though he was a colonel, for some reason he just did not want to order me. I was later to marvel at his command technique. This was serious stuff and urgent. He really had paid me a high compliment and given me his trust. Now that I was willingly softened up, he went for broke.

"How about staying up at one of the division clearing stations and see what you can do up there with your team's primary mission?" At this point the mission was minor oral surgery, full and partial denture repair and replacement, and fracture wiring and splints. There were to be no fillings or crown and bridge work, subject to my judgment.

I laughed again, he was probably right. If we could operate efficiently under forward conditions, we would be on the spot to service the guys who needed those services most. They couldn't easily get back to a unit like this at an evacuation hospital some miles behind them. We'd be swamped at any location, so we had to set ground rules and priorities for each occasion.

"Great." He stuck out his hand, another surprise. "We'll wait until a more stable front for that part." Now, as I remember, he had to be speaking relatively or from understandable lack of experience. Third Army never did have much of a stable front. That was not Patton's way and he damn well wouldn't have permitted it.

One morning, about a week later, a Signal Corps courier delivered orders. I was, "Without Delay," to proceed to the four hundred bed 104th Evacuation Hospital. Map coordinates were appended. The responsibility for determining a fast and safe route was mine. Edwards and I checked with operations for route and conditions and we were rolling in a little over an hour. Case records and partially-finished lab work were transferred to the dental officers of the convalescent hospital.

The location shown on the map coordinates, south

shore of the Normandy peninsula — south of Barneville, was devoid of any visible civil or military unit. There was ample evidence from trampled grass and wheel ruts that one had been there, however. Presumably, it had been the 104th Evac which had already moved, probably toward Mortain along the main line of advance. As I folded the map I'd been studying, a piercing two-fingered whistle came across the nearby field and a GI beckoned. I went over and found a small tent hidden under tall trees.

"I'm Jim Odom, Chief of Surgery," said a pleasant-looking lieutenant colonel as he rose and stuck out his hand. "I haven't had a chance to meet you since you were over in First Army area. Have a seat." He pointed to a folding chair. "The 104th moved up the line. I'll give you the location in a minute. Thought we'd chat a bit." He went on to evaluating medical procedures and policies. General Patton had told him he wanted the best possible medical services for Third Army troops, or as the General had put it; "the finest in the entire Army."

The general realized some doctors spent time in the reserves. Because of this and the understandable haste of their induction, in many cases, the professional man with the higher rank did not have the experience or expertise as one of lower rank. While it was impossible to shuffle ranks around, he made it clear that when taking care of a casualty the doctor with the most training and expertise would call the shots.

Colonel Odom, an extremely well-trained and knowledgeable medical man, had agreed. He said that he had already gone around to most of the surgical teams gathering their qualification cards showing training and background. To their credit, all but a few prima donnas had been agreeable and understanding.

A good example was a surgical team leader, a major with fifteen years in the reserves. He led a thoracic surgery team, but had a limited amount of that type of experience. With him was a younger lieutenant fresh from four years of the latest techniques in thoracic surgery at the Mayo Clinic. The choice was obvious.

"Now, in your case, Vin," he continued, using my first name, "I was a little on the fence. You indicated a first choice of maxillo-facial surgery, but you are also very versatile in other branches. In short, as regards maxillo, you have a hell of a good pedigree, but very little track record."

He paused, obviously, for my comment. I thought fast. He was right. Actually I was not unhappy with the present setup so I said "Look sir, as you say you have my pedigree, you've met me, use me wherever you think I can do the most good. That will be fine with me." His slightly surprised face broke into a broad grin and his hand shot out. The grip was firm. "We'll get along great Vin. I think you're where you'll do best."

In fact, we did get along and very well at that. There was brief small talk. He gave me the new location of the 104th Evac and we left.

At about 1600 hours I found the 104th Evac where Colonel Odom had said it would be. On the west side of the highway to Mortain. The welcome was warm, the first of many. It seemed always so even when the going was rough. By chowtime, we had spotted our truck in the shade of the trees. We unloaded, test-ran the generator, and found bunking spots with some medical personnel.

The rumble and roar of trucks and armor continued unabated throughout the night. This, it turned out, was Third Army's lifeline, one of its main arteries. In a sense, those vehicles were its blood cells. Once we were operational at the 104th you'd have thought we were giving out fifths of scotch. We were swamped. The demand was only limited by the amount of lab work that my three technicians could handle. I could have used a couple more, but that was out of the question.

I couldn't and wouldn't push them to the point of inefficiency and exhaustion. We were up at dawn and worked hard. I usually skipped breakfast in order to take care of emergencies. There were ordinarily several waiting. My third meal was late evening but the men were through at 1700 hours. It paid dividends.

There was Litiborski from Chicago. He was quiet with a sense of humor, and a darn good technician. "Lit" and I did lab tricks that weren't in the book.

Goldberg was from good old Brooklyn. He had a really great sense of humor which he used to mask his fears. He later conquered those fears and became almost gung ho. He was a good, all-around technician; but not a Litiborski.

Edwards, some years older than myself, had come from the backwoods of Georgia. He didn't do well in school and had left after the sixth grade. He preferred hunting, he said. He and I became quite close and must have made an odd pair. The officer with a Harvard DMD and the backwoods man who needed occasional help with letters home. This closeness wasn't accidental. This quiet man had one of the finest philosophies I'd ever come across. He had the innate ability to cut through the veneer and get right to the heart of a matter.

This was true whether the discussion was about our team efforts or on up to international affairs. In particular, our war. His conclusions were invariably on target. It wasn't long before Lit and Goldberg stopped trying to argue with him. Occasionally, he amazed me. I kept thinking, where would this guy be today if he had a good college education? Then I was thankful he was with me right then.

In practical talents, he kept the truck, the generator, and our water heater in good running order. In the area of survival, Edwards had the keen hunter's eyes and sensitive hearing. These came in damned handy later on.

I spent a significant part of the war trying, albeit unsuccessfully, to convince Colonel "Hank" Kind of my parent group and Colonel Jim Weeks to upgrade my guys in rank. I was stonewalled by excuses. The most common was the layers of organization; my bosses had bosses, and on up. I knew that, but kept trying for a technicality or some excuse anyway. The heck with chain of command and bosses. These were my men.

Closing the truck's operations just after 1700 hours brought an immediate development. Major Albanijian of my parent Auxiliary Surgical Group was on temporary duty there. He was a crack anesthesiologist. He buttonholed me fast. "Vin, have you had any training in general anesthesia?" "A little," I said, "some open-drop ether, but with someone watching. I can hit a vein for IV work, know the stages of general anesthesia, and can monitor blood pressure. But that's about it, John."

"You'll do, Vin," he replied. "Look, you know we're loaded with casualties. This Mortain fight is rough, we need anesthetists. You don't have to, but if I break you in and coach you, will you give us evenings? Say, when needed after chow to 2300 hours or so? Just so it doesn't affect your daytime performance."

What does a guy say? "Okay John, show me, but for God's sake, give me extremities." Arm and leg wounds did not usually require as deep a stage of anesthesia as head and trunk wounds. Thus, they were easier to handle.

An hour later, John and I were off in the corner of one of the surgical tents. I got an hour's crash course in intravenous anesthesia that tested me to my limits.

About thirty minutes later, I was slipping an IV needle into the arm of my first anesthesia patient. The big, good-looking, black sergeant lying on the cot had two slugs in his thigh. He spotted the oak leaf on my collar. Though in obvious pain he tried weakly to salute from his prone position. "That's all right, Sergeant," I reassured him, "we're about ready to put you to sleep and get those slugs out for you."

He was from one of our truck companies carrying fuel to a rendezvous with tanks. Though weak, he tried to talk. I let him continue as the surgeon nodded assent. "The krauts were waiting there, Sir. We were sitting ducks. We returned fire but it was lucky our tanks showed up just then," he finished very feebly. We reassured him again and I started the intravenous pentothal. Things went well and it wasn't as bad for me as I'd anticipated.

The sergeant was the first of many.

Something else happened to me that night. It had little to do with the enemy or the war, but it was important. The sergeant had plenty to do with it. I grew up in Holyoke, Massachusetts. Although we didn't have one, we were well aware of a "negro problem" elsewhere in the nation. The high school, with three exceptions, was all white. Yet Bobby Little, a black, stocky extrovert with a big piano-key smile, was our class vice-president and a member of the student council.

Bobby was a "nigger." There were no "blacks" in the early thirties. Everyone liked Bobby, who just happened to be captain of the football team and batted cleanup on the baseball team. Yet, perhaps due to the media, there had been a nagging reservation within me when I left home for college and graduate school. The press and radio reached all corners and the racial virus worked subtly. Negro troops in WWII were segregated.

However, something happened as I carefully put that negro sergeant to sleep that night in Normandy. Over three thousand miles from the "negro problem," that little beachhead of racism died suddenly and permanently, never to infect me again.

The next patient struck the surgical team hard; right in our heart and soul. He was a young GI and an excellent physical specimen. Except now a bullet had crossed his face, taking with it both eyes and the bridge of his nose. We were all new at this sort of thing and not yet hardened to these tragedies.

As he was lifted to the operating table, he begged loudly for someone to get the sand out of his eyes. Gentle restraint was used to keep his hands away from his face. We talked to him as I started the intravenous anesthesia. I suddenly realized that my face was wet. I looked up and saw tears streaming down the face of the nurse opposite me. I felt better somehow. In time, we would learn to accept this consequence of war, but we would never like it.

There was another test to come; the big one. During stateside training, we crawled across muddy fields under controlled conditions. There were little wired and protected explosive charges popping off like Fourth of July salutes. Machine guns fired harmlessly over your head. This was intended to illustrate what it was like to be under fire and, hopefully, weed out the unstable.

It did its job I guess, but I had trouble with it. As I spit out a mouthful of mud early on in the course, I figured it out and calmed down. "I can't get hurt here," I reasoned, "unless I jump up. These guys will see to that. Later on, the enemy may have a crack at me, but not here. I'm muddy as hell, of course, but laundry's cheap." It became fun.

We were now in Normandy however, and someplace, sometime, the enemy was due to take a crack at me. I was worried. The chief part of the worry, curiously, was not that I would be injured. It was similar though. It was the concern about how I would react physically and mentally. The questions of — would I get hit?, where would I get hit?, and how bad would I get hit? — seemed curiously secondary.

The questions were answered late one evening. It was sooner than expected, when least expected, and most dramatically.

Late that afternoon and on into early evening, the Free French Second Armored Division, assigned to

Third Army, had rumbled up the road. They passed by the hospital and bivouacked a bit beyond. We didn't think much about it but the Germans did.

About 2200 hours, I was just beginning pentothal administration to a GI with a bullet in the right arm. All six operating tables in the tent were occupied. This time it was not the rumble of trucks or the clank of tank treads on hardtop. It was the higher pitched whine of aircraft engines; and getting louder, fast. Planes were coming in low. The "ours or theirs?" question was quickly answered as antiaircraft fire of all calibers erupted. The racket was punctuated by exploding bombs not a mile away. Too damn close.

"Take cover," roared the hospital CO as he ran through the bulb-lit tent. It was obviously the first time under fire. Patients were left "as is" on the operating tables about two-and-a-half feet above the ground. The place began to empty fast. The lights still burned.

Reality sank in. I screamed, "Hold it, you guys. Come back here." Three of the last four headed for the tent entrance stopped and turned. "For Christ's sake, let's get these guys on the ground. They've had enough. Give 'em a chance." The four of us ran around and did just that. "Okay, now take cover," I snapped and returned to my patient.

Major Douglas Siefert, the young surgeon, had kept the faith and stayed with him. I looked at him, "Cover," I said, "where the hell is cover? This is an open flat field." He nodded slightly, "What do we do now?" He was prone on the ground beside the patient. His hands were in the air, gloved, with an instrument in one of them.

The ack-ack was intense and the scream of planes

approaching low and fast vibrated the air. I lay down on the ground on the other side of the patient. First I lay on my face, then immediately rolled over on my back as I felt the GI stir. He wasn't asleep. His terror-filled eyes pleaded with me. "Sleep this one out, fella," I thought, and pressed the plunger of the pentothal syringe. He went to sleep.

Major Seifert, though on his back, still had his hands in the air. Maintaining sterility, no doubt. The roar of engines grew louder, too loud. "Tremont Street was never like this, Doug," I yelled. Doug was from Boston.

The scream of engines crested. Another burst of gunfire broke out and stitched a long row of holes in the canvas about four feet above the ground. I'm five-and-a-half-feet tall.

To my shock and surprise I thought, "What a hell of a thing to do to a perfectly good tent." My next thought was, "Jesus Christ those were bullets. Those dirty sons of bitches." Then I laughed a little, I hadn't panicked. I had done what I had to do, what I should have done; and I had controlled that fear. I found something I had wondered if I possessed. Now I knew. "Come what may dear God, I'll hang in there." I guess that was the genesis of the little laugh.

"What's so damned funny?" exclaimed the supine major. "Doug," I said, getting to my feet, the night was silent now. "Do you realize you've been lying there through a near-miss air raid with both hands in the air?" "Holy mackerel," he ejaculated, dropped the instrument, then slowly stood up. "I guess we did all right," he said, "No cover and all that. Let's finish this guy up so we can get him the hell out of here."

The surgical teams and technicians drifted back in

as we lifted our GI back on the table. Doug scrubbed as a medic assembled a fresh tray of instruments. I kept the patient on light anesthesia until he was ready. The arm wasn't as bad as it looked and Doug was both gentle and good. He looked up while suturing, grinning through the surgical mask. I stopped the pentothal, leaving the IV needle in just in case fluids or plasma would be needed. It wasn't likely though.

Doug peeled off the mask and gown. It had been one hell of an evening. I noticed, for the first time, I had been perspiring. I also noticed I was hungry. "How about a donut?" I said. "Lead on, Sir," said he. We headed for the mess tent while the other surgical teams were finishing up. Except for a brief "I wonder if...," we didn't think much about any air raid casualties. Then halfway through the second donut the flood of casualties began.

The German JU 88's had done their job well. In the next hour-and-a-half more than 200 casualties descended on the 104th Evac. A few came in ambulances, but most in loaded-down trucks and jeeps. There were a few French nurses in the medical units and a sprinkling of civilians; local elderly men and women. There was one other, a young boy of about eight years old.

The entire staff worked hard but couldn't keep up with the flow. I became a full-time anesthetist. My wish to work on extremities only became moot and forgotten. Serious casualties were taken first. With a dry mouth and a few prayers I plunged into the battle for survival of the wounded. Time seemed to have taken leave. I couldn't keep track of it.

A bit before dawn, one of the surgeons tapped me

on the shoulder. "Vin, you're a Catholic, aren't you?" Quite puzzled, I replied with a questioning, "Yeah?" "Come on, I have a job for you. Know any French?" "A few words," I said as we walked toward one of the ward tents.

"We've got an eight year old boy here; head injury. He's not going to last long. His grandmother's with him. She keeps making the sign of the cross. She doesn't know yet. Think you can tell her and sit with her for awhile?" Oh Lord, the worst part of the war, the kids. There wasn't a choice, I had to.

In the far corner of the ward tent, one of our nurses got up from beside a cot as we approached. Tears were running down her face. She left wordlessly, glad to be relieved. The medical officer patted me on the shoulder and followed her.

Someone had brought in a box. I sat down on it across from an elderly woman in dark peasant dress. She was fumbling at a large, well-worn pocketbook, head down and mumbling. Her eyes were on a beautiful little boy. His eyes were closed and his head swathed in bandages. I mumbled something.

She was tugging at a rosary twisted around thin, gnarled fingers. Reaching across the boy, I helped her free it from the pocketbook. She surrendered it to me as her eyes searched mine for some relief from her private hell. The worn rosary was very old. It had sent multitudes of pleas to heaven in its time.

Taking the crucifix in my right hand, I brought it to my lips. As I looked at her, I made the sign of the cross and began reciting the mysteries of the cross in English. She nodded almost imperceptibly and joined me in French as she looked at the little, pale face on the cot. We finished the Rosary, my voice having cracked several times during it.

Taking her hand I gently put the rosary into it. She looked at me with gratitude. In halting, inadequate French and rough sign language, I told her the little boy was very badly hurt. I said he would go to stay with God soon and that I would stay with her as long as I could. The tears welled up as she fixed her gaze on the boy's face and reached for his little hand. Perplexing thoughts bounced around in my mind trying to answer the incessant why, why, why? I didn't come up with answers. Over forty years later, I have a few weak answers; most of them uncomplimentary to the human race.

A hand patted my shoulder, a medical officer's. With him was a French soldier, from the French Armored Division. I stood up. "Merci beaucoup," he squeezed my hand momentarily, then slid into my seat as quiet French flowed from his mouth.

The medical officer and I left the tent. The eastern sky was light. It was already dawn.

"Thanks, Vin. If you feel like eating, get some chow and try a couple of hours in the sack." I couldn't eat. I did sleep, barely making the prescribed two hours.

It was 0820 a few days after the air raid. We were already busy. Lit said, "The colonel's coming with company." I looked up to see the hospital CO walking toward us with a full colonel at his side. Even at some distance, I could see the left side of his face was swollen and bruised. There was a trickle of blood from one corner of his mouth.

He was Colonel Kruger of Third Army and chief of all the army's truck companies. That meant he was chief of transportation for food, fuel, ammunition, personnel, and almost anything else moved by truck. His jeep had hit a land mine. Thrown from it, he suffered a wrenched shoulder and maxillo-facial injuries.

It was as the CO said, "my baby." I had him sit in the truck's field chair for an examination. I found a number of tears in the oral mucous membranes, several broken teeth, and various traumatically loosened teeth. In addition I suspected he had at least one or two jaw fractures.

I told this to Colonel Kruger and said there was a lot of work to do. He jolted me when he slowly explained that he had a meeting with General Patton at 1700 hours. He was determined to be there if he was at all ambulatory. This was a very, very, tall order, I explained.

He attempted a grin and pointed at a huge tree several hundred yards away. "My command post for the day will be under that tree. Any time you want me for a minute or longer, you just yell from here. I'll be available." I nodded, "Let's go and try to get some decent x-rays for a starter."

The hospital's radiologist did his best with field equipment that was not well suited for maxillo-facial work. It did, however, confirm there were two mandibular fractures. In addition there was one in the upper jaw on the left side. My men and I had a job on our hands.

The colonel gave a high sign to the radioman in his jeep. It was only minutes before a couple of jeeps loaded with mounted radio equipment pulled in under a big tree. In short order it indeed became a command post. Signal Corps and various other courier jeeps roared in and out most of the day. The colonel seemed quite unperturbed and kept one eye out for a wave from me when I needed him for some procedure.

I sutured mucous membrane tears, removed two fractured teeth, and did emergency, temporary repairs on other damaged teeth. I then fabricated a combined partial denture and splint for the lower jaw and a functional splint for the upper jaw. The problem was greatly complicated by the fact the colonel had to be able to chew and eat field rations. We invented, we improvised, and the colonel patiently commuted between truck and tree as needed.

Along about 1545 hours, things came together. Almost to my surprise the units inserted not only immobilized the fractures, but were functional. He could chew, and several freshly-lost teeth had been replaced. There was mutual delight. Colonel Kruger was pleased and managed a lop-sided grin.

He held out his hand, thanked the technicians and me and said he wished there was something he could do for us. Then, as he turned away from the truck, the still-running, cumbersome generator caught his eye.

He half-turned as he said, "How do you fellows move that generator; with another truck?" "No," I replied, "we get more manpower and lift it up and slide it into this truck. It just makes it, Colonel." "Good Lord that's ridiculous," he replied, "you should have a trailer. I'll see that you have one as of tomorrow, my compliments." His jeep driver had pulled up and they bumped off over the field on their way to the Third Army staff meeting.

My guys were grinning broadly and I was thrilled. It would make us more independent, more mobile, and enable us to carry extra fuel for the generator.

We would even have space for bedrolls and other supplies.

My staff's performance had been excellent. Especially considering that we had taken care of a good day's patient load at the same time. In those days, there were no quick cures or room-temperature setting dental plastics. Every splint or denture requiring plastic was first carved in wax on a model of the patient's jaw. Then we encased it in dental plaster in a metal flask. The wax was boiled out and a mix of uncured plastic was packed in the space left by the wax. This was placed in boiling water to cure the plastic. After being cooled by cold water we removed the splint (denture) from the plaster. Then we trimmed and polished it before going into the mouth for fitting and final adjustments.

Normally, Lit handled metal work and started waxup. Goldberg finished up and flasked. Then Edwards took over for boiling out, curing and digging the cured appliance free from the encasing plaster. We were supposed to have built-in electric hot plates for these steps. However, these units burned out in the first ten days of use and no replacements were available. We used temperamental Coleman-type "white" gasoline burners for the duration. This part was Edward's baby and he was a careful "cook." No wonder I was pleased. I had myself a team.

The colonel was as good as his word. At about 0800 the next morning, a sergeant showed up with a jeep. Behind it was a nice trailer complete with tarpaulin. "Sign here, Sir," he said, and explained that the trailer was signed out to me as an individual, not the group. No one but the colonel could take it away from me. The son-of-a-gun had thought of every angle. "Bolt the generator down," suggested the sergeant and handed Edwards some bolts.

Now we were more mobile on short notice and had plenty of room for supplies and extra fuel.

About a week later, after casualties were evacuated, another evacuation hospital became operational. We were to move up quite a distance as Third Army's armor drove deep into France with all the dash and elan of seasoned cavalry. Traffic on the nearby highway never stopped. Along with the ready rows of loaded hospital vehicles, my men and myself waited for orders to move out.

Chapter 4

ROAD CONVOY

"Major," said Edwards softly. I followed his gaze. Coming across the field was the hospital commander and a energetic-looking major in his forties. They were unmistakably heading for our truck.

As they came up, the major spoke, "You're Major Marran?" It was a question. "Yes, Sir," I countered. "The colonel tells me you're assigned to his command." He didn't hesitate, "I've checked your qualification card at headquarters, it says you're qualified in map reading, also to lead road marches and convoys." He wanted confirmation so I nodded affirmatively. "Good," he continued. "So as not to interfere with combat operations, we've got to move this hospital in four sections. I want you to take the first section."

I was stunned. He produced a map and continued briskly, pointing to a position on the map about seventy miles easterly. "There is a good-sized field here with a line of tall trees on each side. You are to rendezvous here at 1500 hours with Combat Command B-Sixth Armored Division. They'll be in a hurry and will refuel here. Take any casualties they may have." He paused; "Any questions?"

"Yes," I said, speaking mainly to the hospital's CO. "Do I have convoy command or complete command?" There was a marked difference. With convoy command only, I was in charge only on the road and had little or no command once at our destination. This could be a problem and I wanted to avoid it if possible because I had a pretty good idea of what might be needed and how to do it.

The colonel didn't hesitate, "You have complete command until I personally relieve you."

"Thank you Sir," I replied. "How soon do you want me to move out?" "Try twenty minutes," replied the major. I couldn't read his face. Was he serious?

They turned away and I turned to Lit, "Quick, round up three or four sergeants in this section." He left on a trot calling out names. He knew most of them. They came and in a couple of minutes I had my little group. I announced my command status and ordered them to make four specific checks of all vehicles.

1. Check radiator fluid levels.
2. A visual check of all tires on the ground.
3. Each vehicle to have one inflated spare tire.
4. Each vehicle to have full gas tank and one full spare gas can.

They scattered and I moved my truck to the head of the column. We didn't move out in twenty minutes, of course. The major didn't really expect it, but four or five minutes more than that wasn't bad, in fact, it was damned good. We were on our own and the convoy was my baby. I was nervous.

I had also arranged emergency signals in case of difficulty or breakdown of a vehicle. We set out at a steady moderate pace. The timing was important and with Edwards driving I had a chance to study the map, though hurriedly. Occasionally, there was an alert roadside MP with shoulder-slung carbine helping to keep road convoys moving and on course. Army engineers had replaced several blown bridges that had been in service many years. The replacements were testimony to their ability.

Finally, at a major intersection, an MP sergeant and a private waved us to a halt. Our designated route was a good hardtop road leading east-northeast. Off to the right was a similar hardtop road leading due south.

He explained there had been trouble up ahead and that we must detour using the road leading south. He showed us a secondary road on the map a few miles down the road. It led east and would soon get us back on our intended route. I had him repeat the instructions for clarity. I realized he should know the status of the roads, that was part of his job. Yet something didn't seem right. However, I pivoted the column about ninety degrees and started in a southerly direction.

Still, something was gnawing at my mind. I cautioned Edwards to drive at a very moderate speed and studied the map again. As is normally the case on a map, main roads are reproduced in heavier, wider lines. As secondary roads become less wide and less well-constructed, the map lines representing them become thinner and less prominent. This is shown by the map's legend. The southerly road the MP sergeant had suggested was a pretty thin line on the map and its legend.

A little, yellow light began flashing in my mind. "Slow down," I said to Edwards as we approached a side road on the left. It was a fine line on the map exactly like the recommended easterly road. I began thinking out loud for Edwards' benefit as we eased past the road looking at it carefully.

He grunted and glanced sideways at me. I swore softly as the yellow, blinking light in mind turned bright red. If the road we were headed for was of similar construction, width, and on similar terrain as this road we were in trouble. There was simply no way that my heavy truck and the convoy's 6x6 army trucks could get far without being hopelessly stuck in the soft, farmland soil.

I'd rather be sacked for being cautious than miring an urgent medical column in mud. The red light was flashing urgently now. As Edwards slowed to a stop, I swung down from the truck's cab and signaled the column to halt.

About a quarter of a mile ahead was a small, hard-packed area. The tracks of vehicles attested to its ability to stand the weight of trucks. It was as good a turnaround as we'd ever get. I decided to use it and hurriedly explained to a couple of officers in the convoy. Despite the questions and skeptical looks, the convoy turned around and headed back.

As we headed back down the road, several GI's suddenly yelled. I turned to see them looking and pointing back toward where we had been going. I looked back as gunfire burst out. A dense column of smoke rose quickly skyward. I sucked in my breath and exhaled explosively. "Roll it Edward's, but not too fast," I said. I was deciding how to handle that MP sergeant. He had some fancy explaining to do.

As our column reached the crossroad, I was ready and primed for the sergeant and his buddy. They were gone. Instead, there was an MP lieutenant and two enlisted men. A radio-equipped jeep was parked just off the shoulder of the road nearby. The lieutenant quickly approached, I asked him where his sergeant had gone. "What sergeant?" came the reply. Quickly, I explained how an MP sergeant had misdirected us.

The lieutenant's mouth opened in surprise, then he spun on his toes and sprinted about a hundred feet to his jeep. He picked up the microphone, spoke rapidly, then listened for about thirty seconds. There was a brisk interchange. He signed off and hurried over, his face a mask of cold concern. "Krauts," he exploded, "definitely not ours." There had been no trace of an accent, I told him. He nodded, "We'll get 'em, all posts are alerted now. You're cleared to proceed to rendezvous Major, same place, same time. Good luck and congratulations on being so alert." We exchanged perfunctory salutes. I waved the convoy to follow and we rolled eastward.

At 1440 hours (2:40 PM) we reached the rendezvous point, easily identified from both map and terrain. Nobody was there. I elected to use the shelter of a row of fairly large trees bordering the western perimeter and ordered a ward tent set up. Also, two operating setups and support facilities for ambulatory cases and sterilization. There were a few mild protests to which I paid no attention. The virtue of complete command paid off.

We were barely ready when at 1457 hours the roar of engines and the clank of tank and half-track treads shattered the nervous silence.

Combat Command B-Sixth Armored, tore down the road. They wheeled left and in disciplined rows clattered into the eastern half of the field with a choking cloud of dust. The medical half-tracks with their prominent red crosses were nearest us.

They had hardly come to a stop when out of the unsettled cloud of dust I saw two medical officers. I could see their red cross arm bands as they trotted toward us.

With one of our medical officers, I walked rapidly to meet them. The exchange of greetings was cordial, brief, and to the point. One of them spoke, "We've got four litter cases and six walking wounded." I called over my shoulder for litter-bearers. Aid men of the command were already helping their walking-wounded toward us. Without being told some of our men went over to help them. "We're all set up for you," I replied. "How's it going?"

"Good. We'll refuel and keep moving, thanks a lot."

We watched the wounded being brought across the field and chatted very briefly. I wished them luck and they walked rapidly back to their command. The dust had barely settled.

About a half-hour later, the second section of the hospital pulled in. Shortly after that the Sixth Armored Command, having refueled, pulled noisily out and headed east. The 104th's CO came with the third section. By this time the wounded had been cared for and it had been decided they were fit to be transported to the rear. I was very happy to turn things back to his capable hands.

The next day I moved with the hospital up to Etain just east of Verdun of WWI fame. Third Army columns were closing on the fortress city of Metz. For about 1700 years the heavy walls and forts of Metz had resisted attack. It had never fallen. Now it had a reprieve.

Gasoline suddenly became a scarce item. Gas for tanks, trucks, jeeps, and anything that used it was in short supply. Chagrinned and bewildered Third Army units learned with bitter disappointment our gas had been cut off. It was needed to increase the supply to First Army and the British under Montgomery. The medics and the other supporting services ground their teeth along with the combat units.

Only a day following that news I had a young lieutenant from a mechanized cavalry reconnaissance unit as a patient. He was a picture of complete frustration. He said the previous day he and his unit had actually driven into Metz without firing a shot and without being fired upon. The Germans, apparently feeling they could not stop Third Army's drive, had pulled out of the city. Some of its fortifications were even manned by officer candidates.

He had stopped in Metz and talked to several Catholic nuns who confirmed the garrison had left. The fortifications were unmanned and we did not have the fuel to move in and occupy. The distance was too great for dismounted infantry.

This pathetic turn of events was to cost thousands of American casualties later. When we didn't move in, the Germans reoccupied the fortifications and Metz had to be re-taken by assault. The first time in over 1700 years.

Meanwhile, we began to get casualties from our infantry crossings of rain swollen streams west and north of Metz. The weather was unseasonably cold as was the water. Casualties were wet and chilled. Enemy prisoners were stripped of their wet clothes and given dry American uniforms. They had PW hastily painted in white paint on front and back. A serious, if inadvertent, error here caused great complications.

It was mid-morning. I was working in the truck. Suddenly a blood-curdling scream split the air. About seventy yards away was a canvas screen. Behind it was a long slit-trench for latrine purposes. I hit the ground running and sprinted to it as other screams split the air.

As I rounded the screen I saw a GI pulling a trench knife from the collapsing figure of a khaki-clad figure. He was screaming, "My patch, my patch." As I closed in, another GI came from his other side. When I saw he was going for the knife, I went for the GI's waist. The two of us hit him about the same instant, just avoiding going into the excrement-filled trench. Blood was flowing from the back of a GI on the ground.

As the two of us lifted the knife-wielding GI to his feet, we pinned his arms to his side. The trench knife was on the ground and at least a dozen other soldiers were rounding both ends of the screen. Then I noticed the supine figure had PW painted in white letters about ten inches high on his khaki shirt. PW, "prisoner of war." The prisoner soon died. The attacking GI proved to be one who had been evacuated because of chilling and exposure. He was to return to his unit soon.

There would naturally be an investigation. The other GI, who had taken the knife away from the attacker, and I would be the prime witnesses. I kept thinking about the attacking GI's cry of "my patch, my patch." On a hunch I asked to see the shirt the deceased had been wearing. On the left sleeve at the shoulder was the patch of the 80th Infantry Division. This fact made a difference in my mind as I pondered it.

A couple of days later I was summoned to the headquarters tent. An brisk-looking captain announced he was from the Judge Advocates Office. "Strictly routine," he said, "the GI was guilty, first degree murder. We can wrap it up quickly with your statement and the other GI's." He was a young lawyer. I looked over his shoulder at the hospital CO behind him and shook my head in an almost imperceptible negative.

I must admit the guy rubbed me the wrong way, and I didn't like his attitude. Army people have a saying, "The SOB's trying for general first time out." The captain fitted the picture.

So without further preliminaries, I said, "Captain, you'll have to put me down as a witness for the defense." The captain's eyes snapped wide open, his mouth gaped, and his face rapidly reddened. "What!" he exploded when he'd recovered from the last thing he expected to hear. "You, you saw it, you pulled him off, what d'you mean, defense, you're cra...." He stopped abruptly, deciding not to call me crazy. The colonel said nothing, but quietly moved to one side, so better to see both faces. The captain wasn't doing very well in trying to keep from showing anger. That was fine with me, I didn't wait to bore in.

"Captain, that kid did not murder the PW, at least not consciously. You, the colonel, me, and the U.S. Army killed the PW." The captain's face was purplish.

"I'll tell you what happened," I went on, giving no time for interruption. "Our Army took this guy and a million or so others from shoe stores, markets, and carpenter's jobs. We put 'em in uniform, gave them a gun, a trench knife, and made them into killers. For a purpose of course, but we taught 'em to kill or be killed just the same. We sat them down and showed them pictures, big pictures of the enemy soldiers, all types. These were the deadly enemy. Then in camp, on range, and on maneuver, we taught them how to kill. Everything from hand-to-hand combat to the use of various weapons.

"We did something else that has a bearing here. Like the spirit of dear old alma mater, we showed them an emblem. Their division shoulder patch. It meant team spirit, loyalty to the unit, its traditions, past battles won and all that. They were to wear it proudly on their shoulder. Okay Captain?

"Now our murderer, as you call him, has been days in constant combat. Ending up with a few days in cold driving rain on a marshy, swollen river bank. He's evacuated suffering from exposure, spiking a temperature, and probably losing some friends there.

"The other day, getting stronger and with no fever, he's allowed to move around and go to the latrine. Somebody missed his trench knife when he was brought in so he has it with him. At the latrine, taking a leak, he finds himself alongside a khaki-clad guy with PW smeared on his shirt. A Kraut. He bristles, looks again in anger, and sees on his shoulder a patch. His division's insignia!

"Something snaps. Like one of Pavlov's dogs, all the training, all the built-in reflexes are activated. Feeling his division's insignia has been desecrated he strikes screaming, 'my patch, my patch.'"

I paused briefly, the captain was trying to marshal his thoughts, but I didn't give him time. "That's it as far as I'm concerned. Put me down as a witness for the defense." I added, "Colonel Weeks at headquarters knows where I am at all times, right now I have a few GI's waiting." I stood up and looked at the hospital CO, he was keeping a straight face. "You can go, Major Marran," he said. Turning to the captain he added, "The facts fit with what my own investigation found, Captain."

I didn't hear any more as I hurried away. Interestingly enough, I never did hear about the case again, not even to sign a statement. There was no trial, I heard later.

We had a little radio in the truck that I picked up in England. Adequate, but little more than that. Several times an hour the morse code signature, dit, dit, dit, da, of Beethoven's Fifth Symphony, identified the Allied Armed Forces Radio. It played music and worldwide news, highly censored, of course.

I was working on a Signal Corps sergeant one day, the ever-present static was worse than usual. The sergeant grimaced and said, "That's lousy. Want a decent radio? I think I can grab hold of one."

"Sure," I replied, "that's a tough assignment."

"Let me see what I can do," he answered.

A couple of days later, he and a buddy showed up with a six-band Blaupunkt table model. They had a tool kit, and when they left it was nicely installed. They placed it out of the way, up high, and had run an aerial along the top of the truck on the outside. It was marvelous. Asking where he got it would not be the thing to do, so while I wondered I didn't ask. We thanked him very much. "Well," he said, "you guys take good care of us, we gotta take care of you. Yell any time we can do anything."

This is as good a place as any to interject a word on the role of the professional person to an Armed Forces patient. Whether dental, medical, or nurse, it is a dual role. They are both officer and professional person at the same time. In my relationships to patients, I made a conscious effort to sublimate rank and just be a friendly "Doc." Most of my good friends, professional ones that is, felt as I did. Later it was automatic, and it paid off. I felt good about it and when it was all over, I couldn't remember a patient I didn't like.

At one point, I recall getting a letter from my mother. She inquired as to what kind of a practice I was doing. I wrote back, saying that I had the most exclusive practice on the continent. I then went on and gave her a little idea of our function.

Not that I couldn't swing into the officer role when occasion dictated, and feel comfortable doing so. This I did on many occasions involving both officers and enlisted men.

There was one occasion when a dental officer, a captain, demonstrated how not to use officer status. This individual showed up at the truck one day. It happened to be quite warm. The trucks rear doors were open and I was sitting doing paper work in my khaki T-shirt, no insignia of rank showing. The captain's CO had a molar tooth he felt could only be saved by a gold crown. Upon inquiry, the Army Dental Surgeon had told him that I had a centrifugal casting machine which could cast such restorations. It used spinning centrifugal force to put the molten gold alloy into a core. The core was created by burning out a wax pattern, which had been encased in a heat-resisting plaster-like investment.

We were far too busy with everything from wounds and fractures to minor oral surgery to do routine fillings or gold restorations. Nonetheless, I was willing to have one of my technicians cast it for him. The difficulty was the way the captain had it mounted for investment in the investing plaster. It definitely would not cast successfully. In a matter-of-fact, but polite way, I told him. I was about to make a helpful suggestion, when he let me have it.

"Who do you think you are to tell me," he exploded. Instantly, I decided to play it out and see just how far he'd go. He did not realize that he was talking to another officer. So I tried to explain why it wouldn't cast. This time his voice rose considerably and he demanded to see my officer; predicting dire consequences for me.

That was it, I'd had enough. Behind me I heard a gurgling noise that I figured was Goldberg trying to cut off his reaction. Reaching one hand back over my shoulder, I asked Lit to pass me my shirt. I said nothing as I put it on. The expression on the captain's face when he spotted the oak leaf on my collar was really something. His mouth opened, his jaw dropped and he paled to a light ivory. He sputtered and stalled on the first few words. "Oh, Sir, I'm sorry, I'm sorry, I apologize, didn't know you were an officer. Sorry Sir."

Now this remark made me even more angry. He

hadn't got the point at all. I told him so in no uncertain terms. There was no excuse for his behavior even had I not been an officer. I made it clear that my technician was only carrying out the policies and orders of his immediate commanding officer. I added that the technician should have been heard out. Then he could ask for the man's CO for a meeting of minds on the technique involved. I emphasized that I did not like his kind of attitude toward my technicians when they were carrying out my instructions and especially when they knew their stuff.

The captain almost broke into tears and pleaded not to be reported. He said it wouldn't happen again. I really hadn't intended to report him. I felt he'd got the message, but I decided to let him think he'd persuaded me.

Having cleared the deck, the captain made the changes so the restoration would cast well. We invested it and one of my boys cast it the next day for him. To his credit, he thanked me and said he guessed he'd learned a lesson. Naturally, my men were ecstatic and their comments priceless.

There was a light rain falling, it was about 2000 hours. I was in the truck doing paperwork and two of the guys were there listening to the radio. There was a tapping on the door. We doused the lights and one of the fellows opened it with a shielded flashlight in one hand. It was our old friend Colonel Kruger and a captain. "Hi," he said. "May we come in?" They were welcomed and came in. Sensing it was not a professional visit, I made a gesture to the boys. They said goodnight and left.

"Just passing through," said the colonel. "I've got problems and just need someone I can unload on."

"Thank you Sir, fire away," I answered with surprise and some measure of confusion.

At this point the captain, his aide, produced a bottle of choice cognac. I reached for glasses. The aide did the honors. The colonel took a swig and shook his head. "Damn it," he said looking at me, "I'm going to lose some of my best men. They've taken several of my best truck companies." I was really confused now as the aide produced a map which the colonel spread on the countertop.

"Here. Look, Vin. There's a big, important bridge in Holland here at Arnheim," he pointed to the position on the map. "The British," he continued after a pause, "want to force a corridor using two airborne divisions of their own and our 82nd and 101st Airborne. They will then rush ground forces through the corridor. The bridge will hopefully have been secured. Damn it," he exploded, "it won't work, they took my truckers to rush troops though." He verged on emotionalism and was clearly depressed.

While he stopped to refill glasses, the captain interjected, "Major, the staff discussed it along with General Patton and we have decided the odds are very much against success." The colonel's head was nodding affirmatively.

"That's a long way in," I remarked.

"It sure is," the colonel continued, "there are just too many variables. A poor air drop, timing, weather; any number of things can go wrong. This is Monty's brainstorm and one of his worst."

As predicted, the operation was a dismal failure with very heavy casualties. Airborne troops were dropped miles from their intended drop zone. The movie "A Bridge Too Far" eloquently depicted what happened.

Colonel Kruger and his aide stayed almost two hours longer. We talked about many things having to do with the war in general and Third Army's part in particular. The diversion of our gasoline, shifting the supply north to the British for the Arnheim operation had cost us a "walk-in" capture of Metz. Also, it resulted in the failure to close the Falaise Gap.

By the time they left at nearly 2300 hours, the cognac had us nearly crocked. I was in worst shape because I drank infrequently. The colonel got his chance to let it all out to a friend. We thanked each other profusely.

When you are working independently as a separate team, supplies are almost always a problem, at times critical. Substitution, ingenuity, and occasionally larceny help. On one occasion, dental wax for construction of splints and dentures was in short supply, enough to worry me. A couple of days later a box of the needed wax appeared, all without supply slips. Not only that, it was in French-labeled cartons.

"How come?" I voiced.

It turned out that Lit was talking to a non-com patient of ours, an infantryman. "Hey," he said, "I know what you mean, there's a shot-up dental office in my sector, the whole place abandoned." So, we had about twenty pounds of wax just like that. Not according to Hoyle, perhaps, but I mentally thanked the absent dentist for his farsighted supply policy.

We later used this supply method in Germany on a larger scale. With the long and intermittent supply lines stretched out, many items we needed became scarce or impossible to get. My men called the system, "Forward Dental-Medical Supply Incorporated." We showed GI's coming back to us for emergency work items we needed. Sometimes we made drawings or showed small items as samples. When there was a Wehrmacht supply dump or office overrun in their sector, the GI's tried to get some of the items. We found ourselves working with some of the clearing station medics for things they were short of at times. Without it, we would be out of critical supplies. With it, we never ran out.

Colonel Weeks showed up one day. Among the things he had to say was that the Army Medical Supply Dump had run out of prefabricated lingual bars. In order to construct a lower jaw splint, or partial denture, these lingual bars are essential. There simply was neither time nor facilities for individual custom-made lingual bars. A good technician could bend and adapt a pretty good one in a few minutes. With lingual bars, however, we had no other choice, the nearest supply was in England.

Colonel Weeks suggested we try plastic. "Not enough strength or longevity," I said. Then I remembered there was a daily DC-3 courier plane to England. "How about an emergency requisition. Heck, a twenty to thirty pound box of them would fit between some returning officer's feet."

A somewhat dubious look crossed the colonel's face. "I can check, I guess," he replied.

A few days later, I received a courier-delivered message. It read, "Lingual bars can be picked up at Army Med. Dump." It had worked, the whole operation was not according to regulations, but it worked. The staff knew when to wink at regulations.

Chapter 5

FROM GI'S TO GENERAL

I double-timed back to the truck from the hospital surgery tent. Once there I began to prepare a GI's mouth for a partial denture. Behind me Goldberg said quietly, "Visitors coming, looks like brass."

I looked up through the half-opened rear doors. The hospital's CO and a brigadier general headed toward us. Even at a distance I could see the general had a badly swollen and discolored face. I sensed this was a rough one.

"This is General McLean, Major," introduced the somber faced colonel. The general took over, "I'm in a lot of trouble, Major, I hope you can help me. I've just taken over the 90th Division," he continued speaking slowly and with difficulty. He paused, there was obvious pain when he talked. He continued, "I've been to field and evac hospitals. They say my face is all broken up and I've got to get to a general hospital setting up in Paris or England." He grimaced, "If I have to do that, Major, I lose my command. I may never get the 90th or any other division command later."

We were looking at each other eye to eye now. "I appealed to Third Army Headquarters," he went on. "Colonel Odom said to come to you and added that if anyone in Third Army could do it in the field, you could." He was almost pleading now. "Almost all my life young man, I've trained for a command like this. I don't want to lose it. Can you do it?"

I was absolutely stunned. A glance at the colonel's face gave me no help at all. This was a tall order, I didn't dare procrastinate for fear of "chickening out." Apparently I had a reputation to live up to.

"Let me take a quick look, General," I said and asked my GI patient to move back in the truck. "I haven't much time now," said the general as he clambered up and slid into the field chair.

It only took a couple of minutes and I knew this was easily the worst non-gunshot face injury I'd seen. "I'll need what x-rays we can get," I said to the colonel. He nodded impassively, "Then let's take a crack at it and pray."

The general straightened up, "Thanks, son, I'll try to get here whenever you want me. If I can't, I'll see you are notified, just give the messenger another time."

The colonel anticipated me as he queried. "Have you time for some x-rays now, Sir?" "I'll go over with you."

"Yes. Just about," the general replied. Then turning to me he asked, "How soon can you see me?"

With films today, how about seven in the morning?' I replied.

"I'll be here." He liked that.

The colonel looked at me questioningly. "I need an A-P face to film and the best lateral jaws they can get," I said.

He nodded, the general touched my hand and clambered down, "See you at 0700." They headed for the tent where the field x-ray equipment was housed. It was not good for this type of work.

I expelled a heavy sigh and relaxed. This was not going to be easy and the fact that a division command was riding on it sure as hell didn't help. As the GI slid back in the chair, Lit exploded with, "Oh, boy." Goldberg just stood there impassively. Edwards' eyes were closed. He was thinking.

The general was a fantastic guy and had a very good pain tolerance. He needed it. He had multiple fractures of both jaws and a number of fractured teeth and tooth roots. Treating these conditions would be rugged under any circumstances and this man had to command an infantry division.

He also had to manage to eat and come for treatment as frequently as possible. I suggested the mess sergeant chop up his field rations so there was no chewing necessary. I also recommended using a lot of canned juice, although it was infrequently available and not very good.

It was easy to understand why he was popular with his troops. A National Guard officer for years, he related extremely well to all ranks. He and I got along very well.

One day when I intended to remove some fractured teeth, the general came early. A soft rain was falling. His knock on the door was light. "Just checking in," he said to Lit who opened the door. The GI in the chair started to rise and leave. "I can get back later," he said, intending to defer to rank.

"No, son, let the major finish," said the general, "your time is as valuable to you as mine is to me." The awestruck GI settled back in the chair and slowly shook his head muttering a low, "wowww."

On another occasion, a quick call to help on a severe gunshot wound to the face had put me behind schedule. It was pouring rain and chilly. Two waiting GI's were huddling close to the truck. There wasn't much shelter on this day. I didn't realize the general had shown up until Edwards alerted me. I opened the door, stuck my head out to find him huddling with the two GI's. "General, come in we can squeeze you in up front," I suggested.

"That's okay," he replied, "these fellows and I are having a great discussion about this war. I'm learning some things, too."

To every man present, the general suddenly grew about three feet taller, not that he wasn't a pretty big man already.

Much later, I was not surprised to learn how General Patton found the new commander for the 90th Infantry Division. He had marched along a road with GI's of the division and asked them who they thought would be a good division CO. The answer had almost invariably been Colonel McLean. That had been good enough for General Patton. The 90th had been well-trained but poorly led. "Jimmy" Mc-Lean changed that. Not only did he lead well, he gave the division a soul. That made it a great division.

He showed up one day for a splint denture adjustment wearing the two stars of a major general. "You guys helped me get these you know," he grinned.

Occasionally, I got a package from my wife which

contained brownies, each well-wrapped in foil. These were regarded as top secret. Only my men occasionally shared them. This was something special, however. Goldberg had saved some birthday candles from a moldy cake too long in transit. We presented the general with one of the brownies on which were two burning candles. He beamed.

Several days later with the 104th Evac we moved to the Nancy area. We set up on the grounds of a psychiatric compound. I took advantage of a good building equipped with a dental unit. We fed our generator cable in a window and moved some of our lab equipment inside. This was first class, but of course it wouldn't last.

General "Jimmy" came for follow-up of the oral surgery results and the splint dentures. Now a two star division commander, he was accompanied by an aide. His aide was a young captain and he was toting a Thompson sub-machine gun. Not only that, but he held it at the ready and quickly checked adjacent rooms.

I was flabbergasted and opened my mouth to say something. The general touched my arm and said quietly, "Let him alone, he's okay. An over-eager beaver maybe, but he's quick, and a hell of a good shot. He's been told to protect me and he'll be a damn good aide soon." The examination checked out even better than I had hoped for. I suggested he send over one of his division dental officers. I wanted to brief him on what I had done and suggest follow-up procedures.

He said he'd see to it. However, right now he was going to the north end of the Third Army lines to take over a new command, that of Third Corps.

Smiling, he thanked my guys for their part and shook my hand, saying, "I'm much indebted to you. Thanks Vince."

About a week later, Colonel Weeks dropped by. "Nice work on General McLean, congratulations," he greeted the boys and me.

"Thanks, it was sweat and luck," I replied.

The general had gone out of his way cross-town in Nancy to the medical section to praise me quite highly. "Have you heard," he continued, "he's going to command Third Corps, another star in the works." He was all smiles. I opened my mouth to say something, I wasn't sure what. Then I shut it as he went right on talking.

"Not only that, he went to Jim Odom (Chief of Surgery) and wanted to take you with him. He wanted you to administer and sort of ride herd on the medical outfits in Third Corps."

I was thunderstruck. "Jim called me in," he continued. "We naturally couldn't let you go, Corps Surgeon calls for an administrative MD. That didn't impress him. What did was that we had no one to take your truck. Also, as Jim put it, your clinical expertise would be wasted. Jim asked him if he'd want to deprive someone else of the skills that he had benefited from. That did it. He understood then and said, 'Lord no'."

That being taken care of, the colonel came to the real reason for his visit. "About time to try operating with casualty clearing stations," he said. "The 35th Infantry is a few miles east of Nancy. Plan to move in two or three days and keep in touch with me on how it goes." He gave me the orders for the move and a duplicate field order to clear with the 104th Evac.

"You guys get a little rest before you move up," he said as he left.

"Hate to see you leave, it's been good having you. Drop in and say hello when you can," remarked the colonel when I gave him the news. He was good, he was efficient, and I liked him. Three days later we moved out and headed for the 35th's clearing station.

Chapter 6

DIVISION CASUALTY CLEARING STATIONS

The 35th's clearing station was just east of Nancy next to a very old, stone, Catholic church. The division was in a holding situation and the clearing station was well behind the combat line. I sensed, correctly as it turned out, that we were being broken in. Future casualty clearing stations were much closer to the action.

The second day we were spectators at an elaborate funeral at the church. It was well attended by several hundred French civilians, some military, and half a dozen priests. The deceased were two members of the underground, otherwise known as the French Forces of the Interior or F.F.I. They were killed during sabotage operations.

The patient profile began to change immediately. While working at an evac hospital, most of the personnel treated were enlisted men from support units. That is, supply units, ordinance units, trucking units, headquarters personnel, and the like. Now however, the rifleman, tanker, machine gunner, mortar crewmen, and other fighting men were our patients. We were closer to the action. Naturally, they had priority. Officers were referred to their division dental officers or hospital units.

In the midst of these adjustments, a serious and major supply problem developed. Our fuel for the small soldering flames and Bunsen burners was acetylene gas. It was obtained from the army medical supply dump in small, metal cylinders about five inches in diameter and about eighteen inches high. Naturally, we treated this volatile gas with respect.

Now, for no reason we could unearth, this source dried up. We were in a jam. I went to an ordinance battalion. They had the usual large tanks of acetylene about five feet high. However, they could not fill our small tanks from theirs because they lacked proper interconnecting fixtures. The knowledgeable lieutenant colonel I talked with said that if we could use the standard size tank, he would be glad to furnish one. That size would last us much longer as well.

The problem was where to carry the tank. There was very little room unless we stored it laying down under the lower drawers on one side of the truck. The colonel frowned at this. "This stuff can be temperamental, don't do it, could be bad in a crash or a hit. Stand it up."

"How about installing it at an angle, say nozzle end up at 30 to 40 degrees," I asked.

"Sounds better," he said, "the boys can rig a nipple for your burner hoses."

We arranged to bring my truck back to Third Army HQ parking area in two days. There a couple of his crack men and their ordinance truck would meet us and make an on-the-spot installation, if feasible. We rendezvoused with them and they decided to install the tank from the outside. They made a removable hatch so the tank could be changed when empty. I gave directions to begin and left to see Colonel Weeks.

The colonel was dumbfounded when I told him what I was doing. Until I explained. He was still hoping to get the small flasks from England. They never materialized, however, and several other units eventually had to do the same thing.

When I returned about two hours later the ordinance fellows were finishing. They had cut the side of the truck body open and made a hatch so the tank could be loaded and removed. The nozzle end of the cylinder was canted up about 35 degrees. It could then be connected from the inside.

All the fellows were on cloud nine. I discovered it wasn't just because of a successful solution. Just when they had the truck's side opened up General Patton had pulled into the parking area. Spotting the work in progress and the red cross on the truck, he walked over. He took a look and asked if we'd been hit by enemy action. The ordinance men and Lit explained what and why it was being done. Patton nodded, "Don't get hit with that tank in there. Good luck to you and your CO." The men were thrilled to have personal contact with the great Patton.

There are all kinds of battle casualties. There are those due to enemy military action and so-called non-battle casualties such as colds, flu, frost bite, trench foot, and just plain old overexposure to rotten wet weather.

Perhaps the worst casualty, certainly in terms of its personal impact on me, was one I was involved in first-hand when I got a little sick myself.

The cool rainy weather finally caught up with me. I felt rotten and ran a low-grade fever. This was not surprising since I'd been burning the candle at both ends and been in contact with infected personnel. So I stayed in the old house we occupied for sleeping quarters to rest and throw it off in three or four days.

It didn't turn out to be restful or the least bit relaxing.

They brought me a roommate. He was an American full colonel and chief of artillery in one of our fine infantry divisions.

The Colonel had done a brilliant job with the division artillery. Their fire had been accurate and well-timed. Finally, his nerves worn to a frazzle, he sought relief in seconal. He got it from a noncom in the division's medical battalion. That opened the door to addiction. He tried more, and still more, with predictable results. Unable to function he was relieved of his command and treated as a medical case.

I was brought into the picture when the commander of the medical battalion brought him to my so-called sick bay quarters. He introduced us to each other and motioned for me to come out of he room with him.

He told me the story quickly, adding that the Colonel's name had gone in for promotion to brigadier general. It was an almost certain promotion before this happened. It was now out of the question. The probability was he would be sent home as a non-battle casualty, reduced to his pre-war regular army rank of captain, and allowed to resign. In fact, his resignation was close to being mandatory.

Now however, I was asked to share the room with him and be his nurse and confidant. Most importantly, they wanted me to somehow get his gun, a .45 caliber automatic, away from him without a fuss. Since about all the officers in the division knew him, at least casually, they all shied away from the unpleasant assignment. I nodded dumbly and said I'd do my best. I bit my tongue as I thought, "The things this man's army can come up with. What next?"

So began an incredible person to person intimate contact with the Colonel. He was very cautious and wary at first, until I promised him this was a man-to-man outpouring of our thoughts that would not be repeated by me. Then he began to open up. It opened the floodgates to a deep lake of emotion. The clock didn't mean a thing. Quarter hours turned to half hours and then hours as I listened to the outpouring of the Colonel's life from grade school on. The good, the bad, and the indifferent.

I did some outpouring too, much to my own surprise, and found it helped me as well.

To my amazement no medical officer showed up to check on things. I was on my own. Our food was brought to us by a mess noncom. Very gradually I inserted his automatic into the dialogue without appearing to out-and-out ask for it.

Finally, the second evening, after more heart to heart talk, I brought up the gun again. My ground work seemed to have had an effect because the Colonel dug into his gear and came up with the .45 automatic in it's holster. He gazed at it for minutes, then looked me in the eyes and said; "I guess you want this and I think I know why." I'd never mentioned suicide, nor did I now. It was a concern of everyone involved however.

The Colonel unholstered the weapon and, for what seemed like long minutes, examined it from all angles. Then looking into my concerned face he put it on the cot beside him saying, "I guess I'd better not hang on to this. Here it is Vin."

I didn't reach for it, but looked him in the eyes and quietly said, "I rather you handed it to me. You'll feel better if you do." There were thirty seconds of absolute silence. He picked up the automatic, looked at it intently once more, and placed it in my outstretched hand. I shoved it under my pillow and changed the subject to postwar Europe.

The next morning the medical battalion CO showed up with a lieutenant colonel from Third Army headquarters who knew the Colonel well. They were there to take him back to headquarters. The Colonel and I shook hands and he walked to the waiting staff car.

Later, I took the automatic to division headquarters. Then I took my temperature. It was normal so I grabbed a bite to eat and went back to work. A lot less stressful work.

There wasn't much opportunity to observe the enlisted technicians at close range serving as surgical assistants when I was giving anesthesia. Our surgical group had trained them as intensively as possible, courtesy of the Emory University Hospital in Atlanta and other area hospitals. We were able to take them in twos and threes into operating rooms with surgery in progress where they could observe. While observing, a quiet commentary went on for their benefit.

We also went through mock operations back at the base.

Now I would get an opportunity to get back to a supporting hospital unit for a few hours once in a while. Our group's surgical teams knew me and I got a chance to watch them in action. I was really impressed with the performance of our surgical technicians.

A couple of years ago they had been grocery clerks, shoe salesmen, students, and plumbers. Now these amazing guys with no college or professional training were calmly standing at an operating table. They were scrubbed, gowned, masked, and doing a beautiful job as backup assistants. In some cases, they performed duties expected of a surgical intern or resident. I was tremendously proud of them, as were the surgeons.

These unsung heroes have not received nearly the credit they so richly earned. As corpsmen in pre- and post-surgical wards they performed with a competence and compassion that would have left Florence Nightingale speechless.

Several times some surgeon working shorthanded who knew me, would ask if I'd scrub up and assist. If I had the time I was happy to. I most vividly remember a young man with a badly shattered arm. By all of the surgical guidelines and the degree of injury, the arm should have been amputated. The poor guy was pleading not to have it removed. Then he revealed he was a pianist. Standing there as a spectator I closed my eyes momentarily and winced. Tom, the surgeon, was staring determinedly into mine when I opened them. "Got time to scrub?" he asked. I nodded affirmatively. "Go see the colonel. Tell him if he can give me the time, I'd like to try to save it."

I went to the colonel, relayed the request, and told him I'd scrub. He thought for a minute. Finally, he said "Okay, good luck."

While I was checking with the colonel, the young wounded GI had broke into tears. He begged that we let him die rather than have his arm removed. Still very much in tears as I returned I told him we had been given the green light to try and save his arm. He brightened up and his eyes spoke eloquently of his gratitude.

The anesthetist began the intravenous anesthesia. Tom briefed me on his strategy so I could assist more efficiently.

It was a long, tedious, and painstaking surgical procedure. As we finished it was obvious that the prognosis was questionable. Even if the operation was successful the arm would never be useful for playing the piano. You couldn't tell the poor guy at this stage of the game. The belief was that even if the arm was only partly functional, he would learn to live with it.

We prayed this magnificent effort would be successful. Thank God it was not an isolated instance. When time and circumstances permitted, skilled and concerned surgeons would go beyond the parameters of traditional surgical procedures and break new ground.

Another case in point took place in a forward field hospital. I was watching a young surgeon trying desperately to save a GI's leg. The major problem was blood circulation and it looked like amputation was the only resort. He paused and looked up. "If I could only get blood through this severed artery long enough for collateral circulation to develop, the leg would probably be all right."

Collateral circulation referred to the gradual enlargement of smaller blood vessels to take the blood volume of the damaged artery.

"Let's try it," he said abruptly. He turned to a surgical technician and said, "Quickly, get me one of those short glass sippers." It was there in a couple of minutes.

Carefully but quickly he chemically sterilized the five inch piece of glass tubing. He filled it with citrate solution and used it to connect the two ends of the severed and damaged artery. Next, he put a splinting plaster cast on the leg. Then he wrote a brief concise note for the doctors in a general hospital explaining what he had done. For good measure, he drew a diagram right on the plaster cast right over the site of the procedure. If the extraordinary procedure failed, the leg would have to come off. If it was successful, the piece of glass tubing would have to be surgically removed later.

Some few months later, I saw the young surgeon. He broke into a wide grin. "Look, Vin," he fairly cackled, and reached into a pocket. Out came a piece of glass tubing.

"Here it is, and I got a nice note with it. It worked, it worked!"

Somewhere a WWII veteran may still be walking on that leg. With less skill, less dedication, and less luck, he would have been an amputee.

Much credit for recovery of the wounded must be given to the enlisted GI's who staffed these forward hospitals. That surprised a lot of professional medical people. There were only a limited number of nurses to staff ward tents and they had a supervisory role as officers over the GI wardmen.

To their everlasting credit these men responded with a tenderness, compassion and concern that belied the traditional expectations of males. They were terrific. I heard a number of medical officers comment on this. Some said that if they were wounded they would rather be cared for by these young male Florence Nightingales than the nurses.

This is not to say the nurses in these hospitals weren't wonderful; they were. The number of nurses simply was not enough to meet the demands of both civil and military populations. To find young men from the trades and other blue collar origins responding like this was a refreshing discovery in a world at war.

Two weeks later I received a semi-coded field message. I was instructed to report WD (Without Delay) to the Surgeon 20th Corps west of the Moselle river in the Metz sector.

It was early morning so we moved right out and reported to the Corps Medical Section by 1330 hours. Things were humming. As I stood waiting, I studied a map of the area on the wall. On it, in military symbols, were the locations of all the medical units in the sector. They included evacuation hospitals, smaller field hospitals, ambulance companies, and casualty clearing stations.

When a major I knew got off a field telephone and greeted me, I remarked, "I see we're going to crack Metz, Jim."

A lieutenant colonel in the Engineers Section a few feet away jumped to his feet and came over. "How do you know that? Who told you?" he practically spat out.

Astonished, I looked at Jim and saw he was also surprised as well. "Colonel, I simply read this map here," I replied calmly. "There aren't combat units on that map," he answered questioningly. "No," I admitted, "but when you moved in two new evac hospitals; two new field hospitals; a number of new ambulance companies; casualty collecting companies; a forward medical supply section; in addition to existing units; right up close behind the combat line, you expect to use them. Also, you expect the combat line to move away from them. There's only one major objective on that map, Metz."

His jaw dropped. Amazed, he looked at Jim, back to me and up to the map on the wall. "I'll be goddamned," he exclaimed, "makes sense though." The colonel turned away and I sat down opposite Jim at his desk. Metz had not been taken by assault in over 1700 years.

After exchanging pleasantries, he unfolded a larger scale tactical map. "The Fifth Infantry Division clearing station is here at the moment. They'll move up to Pont-a-Musson in a day or two. You can get to them today in about an hour and move up with them." The Fifth was aptly code-named "Dynamite." Captured enemy data testified to the high marks the German General Staff accorded them as an enemy assault unit.

Pont-a-Musson was an old acquaintance of mine. I was first exposed to Caesar's conquest of Gaul in high school Latin. I recalled that Caesar's engineers had built a bridge here giving the town the name "the Bridge at Mousson." The wall map showed it was one of several western approaches to Metz.

Chapter 7

METZ

We found the Fifth Infantry's clearing station on the heights overlooking the Moselle River. They were already striking their tents preparatory to an early morning move to the west bank of the river.

At daybreak we went along with the clearing station and moved into the town. They, wisely, set up in a brick factory building on the river bank. It was a few yards from the ruins of what once was a beautiful stone arch bridge, generations old.

German demolition was expert. Destruction was complete. It was accomplished in a manner that made using an emergency bridge more trouble than building a new one. Army engineers had already put one across about two-thirds of a mile downstream. Despite the swift, flood-swollen Moselle river the infantry had established effective bridgeheads on the east bank. We were busy within an hour or two of setting up.

Temperature was in the forties during the day and

midday and high thirties at night. Skies were grey and the cloud cover was thick and low.

It rained intermittently and the Moselle river was swollen beyond its banks. To further complicate operations, the temperature dropped.

The assault began when the overcast lifted enough to allow an air strike by twin-engine bombers of the Ninth Air Force. Immediately the medical battalion was busy. In addition to the fighting, rain and weather took their toll. Casualties from exposure, colds and flu mounted. My team was deluged but fortunately there weren't many facial gunshot wounds. There were a few facial fractures, but mostly fractured teeth and lost or broken dentures and bridges. Routine work had to go on hold.

The rain got worse and the Moselle river rose above the level of the engineers' bridge. Casualties had to be loaded into assault boats and walked back to our side by GI's, chest-deep in chilling water. Cases of trench foot increased dramatically. In many cases shoes had to be cut off. We had not anticipated this and few appeared to have overshoes. Those who did, and came into the clearing station as casualties, were relieved of them. The shoes were sent forward to other GI's. Our artillery fire extending into the night made rest difficult and led to grabbing quick snatches here and there.

The frostbitten feet and hands had ugly colors, ranging from greys to purples and black. The specter of subsequent amputation in rear area hospitals was not pleasant. Corpsmen worked selflessly as they painstakingly tried to massage circulation into the frostbitten tissue.

At long last, the infantry clawed their way into

Metz. An advance section of the clearing station went in to set up. I brought the next section into Metz with fighting on three sides of us. It had to be done, the chain of casualty evacuation was just too long and precarious. Fortunately, we did not come under fire. The medics worked tirelessly, sometimes around the clock.

Once, during this time, the Medical Battalion Commander approached me. My team wasn't very busy for the moment and the fellows were helping out wherever they could. He said that both medical officers of an attacking battalion had been wounded. Replacements were on the way, but meanwhile he was going to man the aid station. "Want to come along and give me a hand," he said as if it were, "want to go for a soda?"

I went, and for a brief few hours found out what it was like right on the firing line. The corpsmen were superb, many an intern couldn't have done better. The aid station was in the cellar of a stone house that artillery had reduced to rubble.

At one point, I had just finished painstakingly cleaning out debris from a shellfire wound on a GI's upper arm, when one of our tanks rumbled by almost overhead. Loud explosions were heard and the ground literally jumped as German 88 shells hit the tank. GI's tried to see what could be done for the tank's crew. I was swearing as I picked plaster and slivers of wood from the wound I had just finished cleaning. I hastily put several sutures in to hold the torn flesh together and put on a dressing. As I did, three of the tank crew were brought down into the cellar. The fourth didn't make it.

And so it went for another two hours. Finally a

relief medical officer got up to us under fire. The colonel and I waited for a lull, and then got out. My reliable old truck never looked so good.

The bloody battle for the thick concrete forts of Metz resulted in bizarre incidents. Troops were attacking a well-fortified concrete pillbox that just wouldn't surrender. Finally the frustrated American officer at the scene ordered a continuous barrage of smoke grenades shot at the embrasures. Simultaneously a squad of combat engineers sneaked around the back and welded shut the steel doors that were the only exit.

Another remarkable incident occurred as a GI took a break with his buddies. In a sheltered spot he hungrily unwrapped a Hershey bar and tossed the wrapper down the ventilator shaft beside him. It supplied air to underground fortifications. He watched idly as the wrapper sank down and was startled to see a hand reach out and grab it. He thought about it for about ten seconds. Then he took a hand grenade, pulled the pin, and dropped it down after the wrapper. The resulting explosion, he said, even from the twenty feet he put between himself and the shaft was highly satisfactory.

One of the most remarkable anecdotes of the war is the story of Duane Kinsman, an aidman of the Fifth Infantry Division. During the fierce combat for one of the Metz forts he saw a GI suddenly jump up and grab his throat with both hands. He was gasping for breath as blood ran between his fingers. Hurriedly, he crawled over to him. He was turning bluish and was writhing on the ground. The young aidman threw himself on him to keep him still and yelled to a nearby lieutenant for help.

While the lieutenant pinned the GI Kinsman took out his jackknife. Locating the GI's trachea he made an incision below the wound. The wounded man sucked in air in a great gulp. He then took out his fountain pen, unscrewed the cap and bit off the end to make a tube. He inserted this into the incision, and clipped it in place on the edge of his incision.

Private Kinsman had performed an emergency tracheotomy at the height of battle on the bullet swept slopes before Metz.

I saw the wounded GI when he was brought into the clearing station. We all shook our heads in admiration. The wounded GI was in good condition, though he couldn't talk. Word of the nature of the incident was sent back to the Evacuation hospital and spread from there.

Postscript: Private Kinsman, an aidman from a poor family was offered a full four year scholarship for pre-med studies. In addition, he received a four year scholarship for medical school at Western Reserve University in Cleveland, Ohio.

Duane Kinsman became a surgeon, a good one. He's operated numerous times in his career. Still, I bet he'll never forget his first operation.

Working in clearing stations provided a graphic picture of what was happening at the front. The wounded soldiers usually described conditions as much worse than they really were, but dental patients gave a clearer picture. If I wasn't swamped with work I let them talk and get it off their chests. Within limits, I figured it was good therapy.

Occasionally, I could help clarify the situation by connecting the local picture to the general strategy. By explaining how their unit was contributing to the objectives of the overall offensive, they could see they were part of a team. This seemed to help a lot of combatants who, under pressure from the fierce local action, felt isolated from the big picture.

Chapter 8

THE ROAD TO THE BULGE

Finally, Metz fell, and we had a breather. Exhausted troops and medics paused, but not for long. Infantry and armor followed the retreating enemy eastward. They took up positions to regroup, refit, and more critically, to receive a large number of replacements.

The battle for Metz was not as extensive as others in terms of the number of troops engaged. Still, it was very costly in both battle and non-battle casualties. The Fifth and 95th Infantry Divisions in particular were hard hit. With supplies, fuel, and ammunition replenished a further eastward drive would soon begin.

I went back to Third Army Headquarters to report and check on supplies. Colonel Weeks usually chatted a bit, enquired about family back home, then would ask what "he" could do to help "me." This time he was more serious. We discussed supplies. Rising from behind the desk he said, "Come on, I've had you cleared for the war room. I want to show you something."

The war room had one wall upon which was a large map of the American combat front, particularly Third Army's. It was about eight feet high and twelve feet wide. Major American units were in red military symbols, those of the enemy in black symbols. It was December 6th, 1944.

As I studied the map, several noncoms with telephone headpieces made current changes. The captain who greeted us said, "look at Trier just above our north flank."

I did, and suddenly stiffened. Grouped around Trier, the center of a road and rail network, were the symbols of twelve to fourteen enemy divisions. Many of them were Panzer (Armored). "Good God," I burst out. "First Army doesn't seem to be reacting."

"Yeah, Army group and General Eisenhower's headquarters don't believe our intelligence, we're certain of it."

"When they attack, they'll clobber them." I exclaimed. "The staff feel they'll move when we get a heavy cloud cover and low ceiling — nullifies our air support," replied the captain.

"This is what I wanted you to see," said the colonel. "Lets go back and discuss our options."

Obviously if the Germans attacked through the Ardennes, Third Army would have to pivot ninety degrees and dash north to help. Colonel Weeks gave written orders for me and for the Fifth's medical battalion. There was a chance, however unlikely, the enemy would split and drive south in front of us. If they did my orders were to get my team back to the Third Army headquarters post haste. There we would determine where we could best be used.

I was a very sober and worried guy when I got

back to the medical battalion. I gave the CO his sealed orders and told him the day's revelations. We decided to soft pedal things temporarily. Just in case, at the end of the day's work I got my boys to put things in good shape for a quick move. As the days went by, I watched the weather.

A hand on my shoulder shook me awake as a flashlight's beam flicked across my face. The voice said, "It's 0500, chow in twenty minutes. We're moving out, trouble up north." I shook my head to speed the awakening process. "Alert my men," I murmured. "Krauts hit the Ardennes?" The GI was already several sleeping bags away. "But of course," I thought. "Where else?" There was a dark heavy cloud cover.

It was December 16th, 1944. For at least ten days the Third Army staff had pinpointed the attack. Their warning had been ignored by the higher command.

Officers and enlisted men ate hurriedly standing up. Before 0600 some infantry units had boarded trucks and were rolling north toward Luxembourg. I swung into column behind the First Regiment. It was still dark, and misting some. We drove at a good speed, at close interval, and with all headlights blazing. Time was of the essence and both allied and enemy air support was grounded. It presented an eerie picture.

Much has been written about Third Army's remarkable redeployment. It abruptly switched from a front heading east to a dash north. There it hit the south side of the German bulge in the Ardennes. General Patton's forces reacted more rapidly then the German High Command had expected they could.

A number of writers have chronicled how

thousands of combat and supply personnel and their equipment were quickly moved many miles. The Signal Corps strung hundreds of miles of new communications wire. Tons of food, fuel, and ammunition were re-routed as thousands of trucks worked around the clock. It truly was a marvel.

Little has been written, however, about the miracle of the medics in the turnabout. During the critical phases of the battle Third Army suffered about 1200 casualties a day. So skillfully were medical units redeployed that at no time were combat troops and their supporting units without medical support and evacuation. This was a very considerable achievement, and one that saved many lives.

Evacuation and field hospitals split into sections so their patients could be prepared for further evacuation. The other section moved up as close to combat units as caution permitted. Casualty clearing stations with combat units split into two platoons to cover them. Ambulance companies shifted their operations and routes of evacuation as conditions dictated.

At a crossroad I got a glimpse of two radio jeeps, their crews busy at their equipment. Colonel Kruger's, I grinned inwardly, this was right up his alley. Without stopping, and with only a little less speed, the column raced through Luxembourg and on through Esch to the north. A few light tanks with tiny clusters of worried looking riflemen were spotted.

A skeleton clearing station group had picked a brick building and waved me in. The truck loads of infantry seemed to roll by ad infinitum. By early afternoon casualties were coming in. The clearing station was ready. Medical personnel unrolled sleeping bags in very old stone houses on the road leading north.

A couple of nights later enemy night fighters decided to risk flying. They strafed the road blindly. This forced us to move sleeping bags away from windows on the north side. The heavy stone walls were bullet proof, but occasionally rounds would come in the windows.

The Fifth hit the lower shoulder of the enemy's breakthrough. Casualties streamed in. At first in small amounts, then a river of them. They included wounded from shattered First Army units. Medical supplies seemed just to evaporate. The clearing station began to run low and requests came back from forward aid stations. They were dangerously low in supplies.

My men had turned to and helped in the clearing station. Our truck was unmanned and our precious Coleman burners disappeared. They had to be replaced quickly. I borrowed a weapons carrier and took requisitions from the clearing station as well as mine.

The Third Army medical dump was just beginning to get squared away. The harried captain said I'd need two or three endorsements to get Coleman burners. Besides, he added, he wasn't sure he had any. As for the other requisitions, they would simply have to be forwarded through normal channels. I kept my cool somehow and made a beeline to Third Army headquarters, now in Luxembourg.

Headquarters was in a large, stately four-story building. Going down the hallway of the second floor looking for the supply section I heard a piercing whistle behind me. A sergeant, I recognized as

Colonel Odom's clerk, beckoned me to come back. "We saw you," he said, "the colonel said to call you back."

"Hi Vin, looks like you're looking for help, sit down. We'll figure it out," said the colonel.

Quickly, I gave him a rundown of the casualty and medical supply situation of the Fifth. Then I told him about my burners being swiped. He listened. I finished up with the problem of the medical dump. Then I stressed, "There's guys bleeding and in pain up there and this bastard wants stuff through channels. They could be dead by then."

The colonel's face grew thoughtful and he soaked in every word as I talked. "He's overreacting. It's true there have been some false requisitions and a bit of pilferage. There's a black market out there. However this is no time for red tape." He looked pensive. "You're right," he continued. "You're the last guy I'd ever accuse of misuse of supplies."

To his sergeant he said, "Type up in triplicate an order to the supply dump. Tell them to give Major Marran any and all classes of medical supplies in whatever quantities he says he needs. I'll sign it." Turning back to me he said, "We'll give you two copies. Give him one, keep the other to use any time you need it. What have you got for a vehicle?"

"A weapons carrier. I'll load it up," I answered.

While the sergeant quickly typed the order we tied some loose ends together. Then I took the orders and left. "Yell if you need me," he said with a trace of a smile. "You can count on it," I said over my shoulder.

"Medical dump here we come," I said to the driver.

Leaving the driver to swing the weapons carrier tailgate to the loading door I hurried into the supply dump. The captain looked up with an "I told you so" expression on his face. It changed to incredulity after he read the order I laid on the counter. "Call and check with Army if you'd like," I invited with as little expression as I could.

He looked surprised, then ordered a sergeant to fill my order. By this time I had scanned the requisitions and made mental calculations which I decided to supplement. First I got my Coleman burners, resisting the temptation to get an extra. Then I boosted expendable supplies by nearly fifty percent. These are items readily depleted; like dressings, sutures, antiseptics and anesthetics. These were topped off with supplies for our truck. The surprised dump personnel must have speculated as they almost filled the weapons carrier. All this material and no itemized requisitions.

Back at the clearing station the welcome was enthusiastic. Within minutes a generous ration of supplies was on its way up to forward aid stations. The next week was a workout.

Out of a clear sky, I received a message from Colonel Odom to go to Bastogne and check for abandoned medical supplies. Bastogne had been relieved at Christmas. Before that, their medical personnel and supply situation had been critical. Cut off, medical evacuation to field and evacuation hospitals had been impossible.

At a critical point one of our group's surgical teams, led by Major Eugene Reccord, had gone into

Bastogne — in a glider — with medical instruments and supplies. Actually, they had crash landed between the lines.

The team had set up a makeshift operating table in front of the altar in the catholic church on the square. They had operated continually for over forty-eight hours, until General McAluff the commander in Bastogne ordered them to get some rest.

So it was with a feeling of some reverence I walked slowly into the small church and looked at the altar. There were only scattered medical supplies, evidence of the terrific pressure the medics had labored under. We picked up a few boxes of miscellaneous medical supplies and left.

Sometime later I asked Major Reccord what it looked like when he and his team walked into the town square. He asked me if I remembered the movie "Gone with the Wind." "I remember," I replied. He said the rows of casualties lying in the square had reminded him of the rows of casualties in the scene at the Atlanta railroad station.

On the way back to Third Army Headquarters I spotted a GI combat boot sticking out of snow. Nearby, part of a helmet showed through the melting snow. My driver pulled over and we brushed away the remaining snow. We found two American soldiers.

Both GI's were dead. One had a bullet hole in the middle of his forehead. He had four rounds left in his M1 rifle and no other ammunition. The other GI was shot twice in the chest. He had only one extra clip for his rifle. Down in the sunken field below, east of them, were the wrecks of three German light armored vehicles. Two men against three armored vehicles.

It was only a tiny example of what American soldiers had done when the chips were down. Both fallen men had been from supply units. We took the rifles, checked out dog tags, recorded the location, and returned to headquarters. It was a very thoughtful ride.

Throughout the Ardennes there had been literally dozens of tiny Thermopylae's. GI's had simply refused to budge and delayed the German drive enough so a defence, and ultimately counterattacks could be mounted.

Nobody was immune from a good sniper, not even Jim Odom, chief of surgery. Out visiting the field and evacuation hospitals he and his driver pulled over to relieve their kidneys. At about a thousand yards away a sniper lined up the colonel in his telescopic sight and fired. At close range, it would have killed him.

Fortunately for Jim and his strong ribs, the bullet hit a rib from the front and at an angle. It penetrated the fibrous tissue sheath of the rib and slid beneath it along the curved rib. It came out in back where the rib joined the spinal vertebrae. Painful, moderate bleeding, but not serious.

Jim refused evacuation, stayed off his feet for a couple of days at headquarters and continued to function as chief of surgery. He loved the purple heart, handed to him by General Patton personally.

Chapter 9

THE SAAR

At headquarters, Colonel Weeks decided my team needed a partial rest and refit. He sent us south again to the 95th Infantry Division in the Saar area. The clearing station and field hospital were set up in the buildings of a former German Army hospital. The division was in a holding action and business was less hectic. A lot of dental bridge and denture work was the order of the day.

Not that it was monotonous however. One day a single enemy Messerschmitt broke through on a cloudy day and strafed a nearby road. The pilot stopped firing when he saw the red crosses of the hospital. Several days later three enemy fighter-bombers bombed and strafed an engineer battalion that was moving up. There were casualties.

I watched the attack from about three-quarters of a mile away. Having studied aircraft identification, friend and foe, the attacking planes looked like our

P-47 Thunderbolts, and not the German Fockwulf fighter-bombers that most assumed they were. Several officers closer to the scene agreed with me. A subsequent investigation by Army Intelligence the next day did indeed identify the aircraft as P-47's. The Germans had put together the three P-47's from some that had been shot down or crash landed on their side of the combat line. Flown by German pilots they had crossed into our territory without drawing antiaircraft fire. The strafing near us had been the second of two in an hour.

Our fighters normally flew in flights of four. Fighter-bomber squadrons were notified if one plane of a flight went down, the remaining three should cross back into our territory as two aircraft together and a single plane, separated by one half to three quarters of a mile.

At one point, I was drafted for a disagreeable task. A medical administrative major from 20th Corps came and asked me to take a little walk with him for a minute. I sensed something was on his mind, there was. A couple of GI casualties evacuated through the 95th's clearing station had complained back at the evacuation hospital. They said they had been mistreated and subjected to rudeness by medical officers in the clearing station. At first, this had been heard with considerable skepticism.

The next day however a captain was brought into the clearing station along with one of his men. He requested that his man be tended first. Immediately he was assaulted with a tirade of verbal abuse and rougher than necessary physical treatment. At the evacuation hospital he asked to see the hospital CO and recounted the incident in detail. With this further evidence the situation could not be ignored.

The major admitted it was a dirty job, but asked me to find out just who the officers were. He said appropriate action would immediately be taken. When I hesitated, he drove home the clincher. "Suppose your son or brother was treated that way," he cajoled." All I want is name and rank, say nothing to anyone."

I immediately recalled two officers in the mess who frequently sniped at each other. They didn't like each other and weren't popular with anyone else. For a couple of days I spent as much time as I could casually checking in the clearing station. What I saw made me sure, angry, and disgusted. These two officers were engaged in open verbal warfare with each other. The result of this was reflected in rough and abusive treatment of wounded brave men.

I handed the corps messenger courier an envelope with nothing but the two names on a slip of paper.

At 0100 in the morning two new medical officers arrived with the administrative major. They were to replace the two officers who were given three quarters of an hour to get their gear together. Later, I learned that the two physicians received a stern warning. They were then split up and assigned to other units.

Eventually the proximity of the field hospital led to a break in my usual operational policy. One of the nurses, a good looking one, broke a large filling out of a molar. A standard silver amalgam wouldn't restore it for very long. I ended up having the boys cast a good sized gold inlay. This solved the problem.

I suddenly became popular with three or four other nurses who decided they too had dental problems. I fended them off, but resisting the nurse who had been my patient was more difficult.

New Year's was suddenly upon us. Being in a comparatively quiet sector there was a party. It was complete with liquor, courtesy of the German Army's captured stock.

As required, one surgical team did not drink in order to be ready to handle emergencies. I didn't either, but largely by choice. A little while after midnight 1945, a corpsman rushed in to alert the surgical team. He quickly related that an aidman had been on a street in Saarlauten bending over a wounded GI. Suddenly there were air bursts of German 88 millimeter shells. The nose cone or nose fuse of a shell had hit him in the back of the chest and was lodged in the right lung. The corpsman was in bad shape.

When we got to the makeshift operating room, technicians were cutting off his uniform. Without a word the two surgeons began to scrub, and technicians began to set up instrument trays. There was a tense moment. The anesthetist was missing. He was last seen with one of the nurses, someone said. "Find him," barked the surgeon, "we can't wait long."

Then he spotted me, "Open drop ether. You've got to start induction, Vin." I nearly collapsed, this was way over my head. I was just plain frightened. I opened my mouth to protest but he beat me to it. "I know, I know, just get us started. We'll find him."

I started with the GI resting on his side. He would be on his stomach after induction and a tube placed in his larynx. I was cursing the absent anesthetist to myself. With some coaching, the induction went pretty well. Just about the time we should intubate, the red faced, apologetic anesthetist ran in, somewhat out of breath, and took over. A heavy weight was lifted from my shoulders, and I became a concerned spectator. A praying one I might add.

Well over an hour later, the bloody nose cone with fragments of bone and tissue on it was removed. Vessels were tied off, tissue closed, and drains put in the back of the chest. The GI's condition was very critical. He was later evacuated in guarded condition. Because he was a medic we all felt a kinship with him and prayed he'd make it.

Our patients were not all American soldiers. The enemy had wounds needing treatment also. Walking-wounded German prisoners had a GI or two, usually MP's, sent with them to the casualty clearing station as guards. One day it was "standing room only" in the station. I went in several times to lend a hand.

The fourth time I walked in, I stood in the entrance for a minute, surveying the seated wounded lining the walls. There were five German soldiers seated along one wall. To my surprise, the escorting guard was seated opposite them about seven feet away with arms folded. His carbine was leaning against the wall near one of the Germans. The prisoner was slowly sliding down the bench toward the rifle. Without a word I swept across the room and scooped up the carbine with one hand.

Then I turned to the guard and reprimanded him in no uncertain terms. "Aw Major, I had the bastard cold," he revealed a small automatic in his right hand. Then I really blew up. "You fool, do you want to make a shooting gallery out of this place?" I was damned angry. He said his carbine wasn't loaded. However, it would have made a good club and the prisoners could have managed to conceal trench knives. The only logical choice was to put him on report. I did.

It was almost mid-January when the messenger courier handed me new orders. We were going back up north to the Fifth Infantry Division. There was still heavy fighting as the "Bulge" was being reduced.

As we drove away from the 95th's clearing station, Edwards remarked, "That gal's a mighty pretty woman, mighty pretty."

"Yeah, but I'm married," I rejoined. "She's a looker, though," he insisted.

"You should've spoken up earlier, maybe I'd of let you take my extra set of oak leaves," I went on. "Well, I can handle 'em, but not that high class stuff," was the grinning reply.

We found the Fifth's clearing station east of Luxembourg, in the shadow of the old Radio Free Europe station. We were immediately busier than I had expected to be. There were few fractures, but a great many lost and broken dentures and bridge work. Under the harsh conditions of long combat, a lot of filled teeth in poor condition had broken down. Many of these GI's were hurting. There's nothing like a severe toothache to make you ineffective.

Chapter 10

OPERATIONAL POLICY

Now that pressure on the division was off, some officers of the Headquarters' staff were getting passes to Paris. This had an unfortunate effect on me.

I was approached by the medical battalion commander and two other officers. They wanted me to do complex crown and bridge work for a few high-ranking officers. They discovered we had the necessary equipment. I politely refused, saying it was contrary to Army policy. Moreover, I was snowed under by urgent work on frontline GI's who could hardly eat. "Besides," I pointed out, "officers of that rank can easily get to fixed installations where the work can be done easier, and probably better."

As the pressure mounted my resistance stiffened. Their threat of "going to Army" left me unmoved. The conditions in the mouths of many forward combat men lent strength to my resolve.

In addition, I had in my pocket a note from a

forward company commander. The captain asked me if I would please do something for a sergeant who was his good right hand. He got nowhere, he wrote, with the clearing station dental officer. The sergeant himself had shown up at the truck a few days earlier with the note. I had been appalled at the very bad conditions in his mouth. I had promised him I'd help him and had scribbled an anonymous note for him to give to his captain. I kept the captain's identity confidential.

Somewhat to my surprise the medical battalion brass did complain to Colonel Weeks. They returned saying they had been given an okay to have me "cooperate." I didn't believe it, knowing Colonel Weeks as well as I did. After further discussion, they revealed that Colonel Weeks response to them was that my attitude was "policy." Still, if I felt it would not interfere with my primary mission he would not object. I laughed inwardly, the bugger knew me and was throwing the ball back in my lap. So I still politely said no.

Now the colonel tried a new tack. "You know," he said, clearing his throat, "we have several Bronze Stars available for presentation to attached personnel. If you'd just be reasonable, one could be yours."

That did it. I exploded! If he put that Bronze Star where I told him to, he'd need the services of the nearest proctologist. At that instant, I knew I'd blown it. The colonel reddened and the other two officers stood there, mouths agape. In the second before he could lower the boom there was a loud knock on the door. Someone opened it. A voice said, "Urgent phone call for Major Marran at the message center. Third Army calling."

"I'd better take it," I murmured, wondering if it was good or bad. The colonel, beet red, nodded.

"Marran here," I said into the phone at the message center.

The voice that answered was Colonel Weeks. "I had visitors from the medical battalion this morning. What the hell's going on?"

I told him, including the note from the captain. "I thought so," he replied, "I was stalling for time to get to you when I bucked it back to you. You're right of course. How are you going to handle it? Need help?"

Then I told him about the Bronze Star bit and my big mouth. "Oh God," he said, "I can understand your slip, those medals are for brave men, not bribes. Don't worry he's not going to lay a hand on you. We'd better get you out of there though, there are several divisions screaming for your services. I don't know which one I'll send you to now, but immediate action orders will be on the way to you in an hour. Turn your cases over to someone and get ready to roll. Good luck. Keep your shirt on, fella."

We rang off. Demurely, very demurely, I returned to the colonel and notified him I was under orders to move. The colonel simply nodded his receipt of the news. I suspected that in my absence the idea of using a medal for a bribe was discussed. I got the impression they'd rather forget it. Anyway, there was no comment. I left to get the truck ready to pull out with mixed feelings, but damn grateful to Colonel Weeks for his understanding and support.

Our orders arrived by special courier in several hours. Cases had been transferred to the clearing station. The incident with the medical battalion officers had obviously been spread around. I politely declined comment.

There was still a little daylight and I decided to put some mileage behind us. I picked out an evacuation hospital on the map where we could stay overnight. The orders were to the Fourth Infantry Division then nearing the Siegfried Line. The orders further added, "Check with Third Corps." This meant that Third Corps would give us directions on getting to the clearing station. The weather was heavily overcast.

We left the evacuation hospital next morning and over terrible roads got to Third Corps headquarters at midday. The welcome was warm and they saw to it that we had a hot meal. After eating, out came the map and they plotted the latest clearing station location. We discussed the best route to it.

The problem was the very muddy condition of the roads. Some were impossible for heavy trucks. Engineers were frantically working on them so constant update was in order. We started on a road that looked like a fair bet to get us through. On the way there we were stopped by engineers. They told us the road from there on was a sea of mud. I checked the map looking for possible alternatives. Then I spotted a single track railway line the map showed would bypass the quagmire, if we could use it. As I looked at the terrain a crew started to rip up the rails from the roadbed.

Great, someone else had thought of it as well. Checking with the detail's sergeant, I swung down onto the roadbed determined to follow along at their heels. There were a couple of mine detector crews around so I asked one of them to sweep ahead of the truck. They thought it was a good idea, so the procession went along ripping up rails and sweeping for mines. My truck was close behind as we proceeded at a snail's pace. Nonetheless, we were moving.

This did get us to a better road. From there I elected to take a ridge road that logically would have to be dry. We barreled along this road a couple of miles until frantically waved down by a lieutenant. Some other trucks had tried that road in the last two hours, he said. They had been blown off the road by artillery fire. It was in plain sight of enemy batteries several miles away. To go or not to go, the choice was mine. What the hell, they said we were needed.

Solomon sponged off the red crosses on that side of the truck. We refreshed our memories on "ditching for cover" procedures. Edwards took the wheel and we tore down the road. There was no gunfire from the German artillery.

As things turned out, we ended up driving back from the front to division headquarters and the clearing station. As we did it was raining supply parachutes over a big field adjoining the road. Ground transportation of supplies was too risky. When we finally arrived, they were both surprised and glad to see us.

Chapter 11

PRUM AND THE SIEGFRIED LINE

We set up the clearing station in absolutely the muddiest conditions imaginable. This was Prum, Germany. Just to the east was the Siegfried Line. Very quickly an excellent and friendly working relationship emerged with clearing station personnel. Business, if you could call it that, was quite brisk.

The division pushed through Prum and into the Siegfried Line. We followed. Prum was an absolute mess. Most buildings were destroyed by artillery and deep mud was everywhere. There was something else. The smell. The sickening odor of putrefying flesh from bodies in the rubble filled the air. It was the first experience for me, but not the last.

The medical column continued through to an old abbey in the hills east of Prum, where the clearing station was set up. The boys carried my sleeping bag up a flight of stairs and dumped it in an outside room facing east. I went up to check. There was an old iron cot in the room. I unrolled the sleeping bag on it and walked to the window.

Below me, hidden from ground view by bushes and tall, untrimmed grass, were the bodies of five GI's who had died storming the defended abbey. I called down to several medics nearby and directed them to the bodies, then went down to help. We took their rifles, checked out dog tags, and tenderly removed the bodies on stretchers brought from the stations's supply. Some casualties were already coming in as darkness closed in with a rush. I was bushed.

The CO saw my fatigue and suggested I take a seconal and turn in early. I did. It was the first and last time. Sometime during the night I was partially aroused by a banging and clattering nearby, but went back to sleep. Shortly after dawn I awoke and wiggled out of the sleeping bag. I was partly dressed, so I walked to the window for a breath of fresh air. Instead, I froze and remained rigid! Balanced precariously on the window sill was a 105 millimeter shell. It had landed there during the night and not exploded.

I grabbed shirt and field jacket and made my way unsteadily down the stairs to the mess. The CO took one look and said, "you look awful, what's the matter?" I told him. There was a dead silence at the table. A GI ran up and checked. "Call the ordinance bomb boys. I can hardly believe it," he said as he came down the stairs.

I had heard of duds, but this one balanced on a window sill, even one of thick stone, had to be something of a record. Ordinance felt it had hit somewhere just east of the abbey. It must have ricocheted, then hit and bounced from side to side in the heavy stone window opening. I wasn't listening. There was no such thing as luck. God did it. He had a plan, I was in it somehow. My prayers were very long that night.

The Prum-Siegfried Line conflict began easing off some. I had to go back to Third Army headquarters in Luxembourg for routine reports. Captain Ippolito, one of the Fourth Division's dental officers, told me he had become good friends with a druggist there named Hurt. The captain had stayed overnight with him and his family and enjoyed their hospitality. He suggested I contact him.

I brought my men back with me. We usually stayed overnight at one of our hospitals in or around the city. This time I checked at headquarters to be sure it was all right, for me to stay with the Hurts. It was fine, they said. So I looked up the druggist at his modest drug store.

I was treated like a long lost friend. It took little persuasion for me to agree to have dinner with his family. Besides he and his wife, there were two young children; a boy and a girl. During the German occupation, the children were held hostage to prevent any action by them in the underground. It was a remarkable family.

I must stay the night, they insisted. I did, although somewhat embarrassed because of having gone without a shower for days. My uniform, my cleanest at the time, was no bouquet of flowers either.

After an evening of pleasant conversation, they suggested I retire early. The "guest room" bed was turned down and clean pajamas, towel and washcloth, lay invitingly on it. Sleep came in minutes after a shower, and it was a good sound sleep.

When I awoke about seven the next morning, I was speechless. The chair where I had carefully put my filthy clothes now held spotlessly clean, ironed and folded clothing. Stockings, underwear, shirt, trousers; everything was immaculate. To this day I don't know how Mrs. Hurt performed the miracle. Yet perform it she did, this time and couple of times later. Each time she would shrug off my thanks with a smile.

I spent several evenings with guests from the University of Luxembourg. It taught me much about the Europe we had come to liberate and what to expect after hostilities.

The division did its job and penetrated the Siegfried Line. They were then pulled out of combat. Not just for a rest, but to be sent south to the Seventh Army area. Since we were Third Army personnel that automatically detached us. We packed and returned to our group headquarters for further assignment.

Several surgical teams were also there for brief rest and reassignment. Liquor, courtesy of the German Wehrmacht, and French cognac was available and they were relaxing. The "relaxing" progressed. In fact three or four men overdid things the second evening. It got out of hand about midnight.

The most agile of the group decided to imitate a baboon. Having stripped, he proceeded to demonstrate the awkward waddling gate of the species. There was a hilarious acceptance from his buddies. Encouraged, he climbed the tent pole. Bathed in the beams of two or three flashlights, he supplied his own sound effects. The group CO was patient and understanding to this point.

Author in England moments before boarding LST for beaches of Normandy. (see Chapter 2)

Author's medical truck being washed from stream using gasoline powered pump.

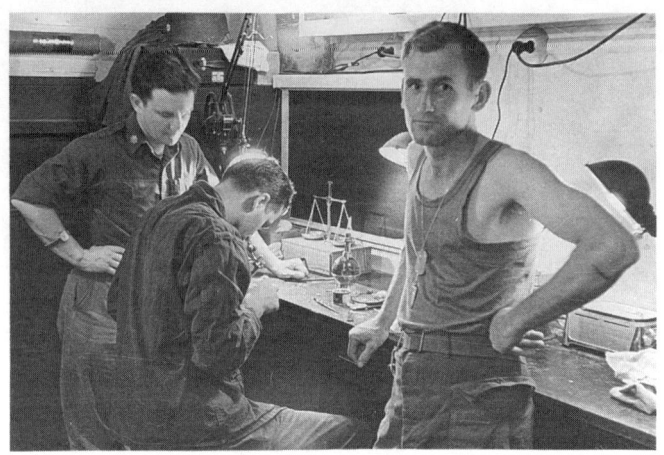

Author (left) inside truck with technicians Litiborski (center) and Edwards (right).

Author (right, with red cross on arm) examining route to move up behind combat troops.

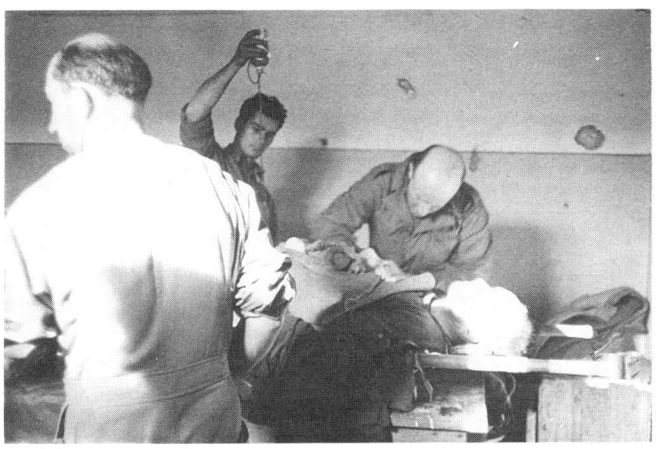

GI on litter received chest wound in attack on Metz. Enlisted medic holds plasma as surgeon tries to save life of patient who had quit breathing. Patient began breathing and was given a good chance to live. (see Chapter 7)

Tank moving into battle. Infantrymen frequently rode tanks until enemy was engaged, then drop off and deploy. Note Goldberg sticking his head out of author's truck at bottom left. GI on tank facing him quipped, "Is this the road to Berlin?" (see Chapter 11)

American GI's killed in attack on an Abbey just east of Prum, Germany. This battle was part of the attack on the Siegfried Line. (see Chapter 11)

Strakonitz, Czechoslovakia. Russian General and two staff officers getting out of jeep (center of photo) as townspeople look on. They had come to see if Americans had "everything under control" (see text, Chapter 17). Tank at left is from 4th Armored.

Author (center — bareheaded) with Russian soldiers. Russian female assistant and medical officer sitting on author's immediate left (see text, Chapter 17).

Surrendering German troops with some German civilians. Strakonitz, Czechoslovakia; May, 1945.

What followed was probably inevitable. He decided to urinate. From the top of the pole. The light yellow stream reflected brightly in the flashlight beams as it fell, directly on the head of the group CO.

I quickly retracted my head like a nervous turtle, as if it would shut out the imminent eruption. It didn't, and the resulting tirade was well deserved.

The next day, Colonel Weeks sent over three-day passes to Paris for myself and my men. We locked up the truck, grabbed some gear and caught the Paris leave train from Luxembourg. The glorious R&R included the Follies, the Louvre, Notre Dame, and other magnificent sights of Paris. Afterwards, it was the slow night train back to Luxembourg. There were no sleeper cars, but we didn't mind after our superb leave.

Orders were waiting for us to report to the 76th Infantry Division clearing station. We joined them as the division was driving toward the Rhine. There had been strafing that day by the nearly dead Luftwaffe. I took my hint from the foxholes near the personnel tents and figured I'd better follow suit. I was struggling with the top foot of packed earth when a voice said, "Sort of reminds you of the WPA don't it." I looked up. A big smiling GI was putting his rifle down.

He reached for the shovel, saying, "Let me do it sir." Gratefully, I sat down. I was amazed at the rapidity with which a generous sized foxhole appeared. The GI wasn't half as winded as I was just watching him. I thanked him and we gossiped for a few minutes.

He said he'd heard that some strafing planes had something called jet propulsion. They were so fast, he said, that fifty-caliber antiaircraft guns had not been able to be effective. It sounded a little far-fetched, but it proved to be true. Late in the war the German scientists did develop the first military jet aircraft and a few did get into the air.

The next day a sergeant from one of the mechanized reconnaissance outfits came in with problems. These recon squadrons were Third Army's eyes and ears behind enemy lines. This group was commanded by a very young West Pointer who was becoming a legend with his group.

As I worked, we chatted a bit. I asked the sergeant just what kind of a guy their commander really was? His answer deeply impressed me. "I'll tell you something," he said calmly. "If we were ever in a situation where he was going to be shot — and I could lunge in front of him and take the bullet — I wouldn't hesitate a split second. That tell you somethin'?" The young lieutenant colonel was a very rich man, I thought. I hoped he'd make it through the war. We needed men like that.

A courier dropped off our mail periodically. This time there was a note from Colonel Kind. Major Fonde had been killed. Fonde had been chief of a crack surgical team of our group. In addition, he had done so well in an executive capacity he had been scheduled to command a field hospital. Colonel Kind's note said that he had been moving up a section of a field hospital following a combat command of the Fourth Armored.

He apparently had misread the map and was stopped by an SS lieutenant and an SS sergeant. It was drizzling. When motioned to get out of the jeep, he reached down to pick up the lower part of his raincoat. The blast from the sergeant's submachine gun nearly cut him in two killing his driver as well. Despite the fact the entire unit was clearly a medical unit and included several nurses, the SS unit took them prisoners, medical equipment and all.

It wasn't according to the Geneva Convention of course, but that didn't stop the SS. When they heard about it the officers and enlisted ranks of the Fourth Armored reacted angrily. A rumor circulated that the nurses had been molested. This further incensed them. They attacked savagely and weren't particular about taking prisoners.

Cooler heads in the Wehrmacht got the message and all medical personnel were returned under a flag of truce. Vehicles and medical equipment, however, were not returned. This too was a violation of the Geneva Convention. The returned prisoners all reported they had been well treated.

I felt very badly about Ed Fonde. I had met his wife and three small children during training back in Georgia. I felt badly too for another reason. During our training I had given the map reading classes for our group's officers. Ed just wouldn't take them seriously and skipped lectures. He reasoned that medical groups would be shepherded around so why bother. Try as I did, I couldn't convince him otherwise. If he had taken map reading seriously, he probably would not have taken the wrong road and ended up killed by the SS. I brooded over it for a while, and then laid it to rest.

Chapter 12

THE RHINE

The 76th closed on the Rhine and the engineer bridging battalions moved up.

On Good Friday, along with the clearing station, we crossed the Rhine on a pontoon bridge at Saint Goar. The column following the trucks of infantrymen swung north through a small town and its town square.

Two MP's stood at the flagpole taking down the Nazi flag. They carefully snapped the stars and stripes to the pole's halyard and began to raise it. The column halted without a word or gesture of command. All hands left their vehicles, snapped to attention, and saluted as the flag was raised. More than anything else, this tells a lot about those American troops. Years later I still have a feeling of great pride when I recall that incident.

The next day there were two serious maxillo-facial casualties. I decided to ride back to the evacuation hospital in the ambulance and keep an eye on them. I wanted to report to Colonel Weeks as soon as possible anyway. There was another, not very serious casualty, and an infantry captain with two machine gun slugs in his thigh. He was fairly comfortable, if it's possible to be comfortable in those ambulances.

It was the habit of the ambulance drivers to adorn their vehicles. They did this with photographs of luscious women placed for the edification of themselves and their wounded passengers. This particular driver had done well indeed. I was admiring a beautiful semi-nude young lady when I noticed the captain's eyes practically devouring her. I couldn't resist saying "What do you think of her?"

"I'll tell yuh," he answered in a flash, "I'd eat a yard of her shit just to see where it came from." Two of the three other casualties made appreciative noises. I didn't attempt to stifle an exclamation. Going from the earthly to the sublime, he looked at me and continued.

"I've got a beautiful wife and two small girls at home. I've been thinking. You know, it's really not important if we get home. If we get our job done here what really matters is that they will be safe and warm and taken care of." We chatted the rest of the way back to the hospital. It was one of the more memorable conversations I've ever had.

We moved up every few days as Third Army drove deeper into central Germany. The medical units quickly adjusted to th new situation in order to keep as close to the wounded as possible. Division clearing stations activated their two platoon organization.

The two platoons operated independently of each other. One clearing platoon received and treated casualties while the other leapfrogged it as the combat line moved forward. They then set up close behind the combat units. As soon as the first platoons casualties had been evacuated they packed up their equipment and got ready to leapfrog the platoon at the front. This was possible because the battle had moved on by then. When one platoon finished before another there were often short pauses between movements.

It was during one such pause that I noticed something. On a nearby hilltop was an impressive four-story monastery, complete with a tower. It was similar to the dozens of active monasteries that once dotted hills in Germany. Then I noticed a large, very faded red cross on the big sloping roof. I went to the platoon commander and suggested it might now be a military hospital and should be checked out. There might be German wounded inside, and perhaps some wounded Americans. Agreeing, he called to a nearby medical officer and asked him to go with me.

As we drove up to the imposing entrance in a jeep, two unarmed German soldiers saluted us. Then one went into the building and came back with a medical officer who greeted us in fairly good English. He readily agreed to take us through the wards and sent for the commanding officer, a lieutenant colonel.

I had noticed immediately the building had a very unpleasant odor. The commander explained that medical supplies had run out days ago. Dressings were unchanged for days and they were now using paper for bandages. Antiseptics were almost gone as well. When we asked to see the patients, and in particular any American patients, he willingly complied. Eleven of the 160 to 170 patients were Americans.

They, like the German patients, were also without

proper dressings and in need of medical supplies. However, they said they had been as well cared for as the Germans. Naturally, they wanted to get back to American hospitals. We spent some more time inspecting. When we left we assured the German CO that we would make sure our medical supply units were apprised of the situation. We felt certain they would help if at all possible.

The captain and I reported to the clearing platoon commander. Field messages were sent by courier requesting several medical officers and ambulances to evacuate the American wounded. We also requested that every attempt be made to get medical supplies to the German hospital.

Early the next morning our clearing platoon moved up. We were subsequently notified that our GI's had been evacuated, and medical supplies were being sent to the German hospital.

Edwards had just cranked up the generator one morning when a medical and a dental officer of the clearing station showed up. A staff sergeant and his buddy from the division's tank battalion were with them.

The left side of the sergeant's face was swollen up about the size of half a small grapefruit, and quite red. A lower impacted third molar had become infected and infection had rapidly spread into the facial tissues. Under operational guidelines for this type of infection he should be sent back to a hospital. However, the sergeant wasn't buying that idea one bit. He just did not want to go back, period.

It occurred to him that I outranked the captain he was with and he insisted on seeing me. The officers were sure I would echo their decision. After examining him I concurred with them. I explained why it was the best thing for him. He listened and then asked me to hear him out.

His unit had driven into enemy territory without waiting for replacements. The strength of the tank battalion had been whittled down to twelve Sherman tanks. The sergeant was the ranking man since all officers were either killed or wounded.

At this point, his buddy, also a sergeant, took up the argument. He explained that, like a football quarterback, the commander for the attack called the formations, tactics, and targets by radio. The staff sergeant was the ranking man in the twelve tank crews. As such, he was the only one with good knowledge of the tactics and verbal command signals. Both sergeants pleaded with me to perform a minor miracle.

I was very much impressed with the sergeant; both his bearing and attitude. So while the two officers expected me to order evacuation, I was thinking deep and fast. I would have to make one difficult deep injection. It would reach the sensory nerves to the face and jaws where they came out of the base of the skull. It was little used because general anesthesia was preferred. However, that was out of the question.

As I say, I was impressed by the sergeant. He wanted to lead his tanks against a superior group of eighteen enemy tanks at dawn the next day. So, after exacting promises of absolute cooperation from both sergeants, I decided to go for broke.

It was clear the medical and dental officer had a negative view of the situation. Nonetheless, I made preparations and arranged for Lit to assist me. The injection was a success, thank the Lord. The sergeant got good anesthesia on the left side of his face. A copious amount of pus oozed from the wisdom tooth area when drainage was established. I let it bleed to irrigate the area. Then I packed the resulting wound with a large amount of iodoform gauze drain impregnated with sulfanimide powder.

Throughout the surgery the sergeant had sat without moving a muscle. After carefully suturing the wound I launched into dogmatic and detailed post-op instructions to both sergeants.

I made his buddy, who would be in the tank turret with him, my assistant. He was to supervise medication. I gave him a supply of sulfadiazine tablets with dosage orders. The sulfas were apt to be rough on his kidneys, so I had Solomon round up three extra canteens. I gave strict instructions. Almost every time the patient opened his mouth he was to drink at least a third of the water in the canteen. I admonished him to do this even if he had to wet the floor of the tank.

After giving some aspirin for pain I gave them a clinical thermometer. I insisted that if the fever rose above 100 degrees that they promise to throw in the sponge. I made them promise to get back to the clearing station pronto. They promised, and I was satisfied they meant it.

As they walked away the medical officer shook his head, "I hope it works," he said.

We all knew if the Shermans could handle the German tanks there would be considerably fewer infantry casualties in the coming attack. It is difficult to expect God to take sides in a situation like this. However, that night I asked him to, for the sergeant and his men.

It was early dawn when I was awakened by the distinctive bark of our 105 howitzers. A little later the sharper report of the tank's 75s joined in. I was as nervous as if I had been there. It began an uneasy day. The clearing station received a few casualties. They reported the attack was successful, but didn't know much about our tanks.

About 1530 hours, I spotted the sergeant and his buddy walking toward the truck. Even at a hundred feet I could see the swelling of his face was appreciably less. He was attempting a smile. I greeted him with, "Get up here. Let's take a look."

Strangely, neither sergeant said a word as he sat down in the field chair. He was holding a moderately sized brown package in his lap. Indeed the swelling had decreased and the tissues looked less angry. I removed the gauze drain, irrigated the area and placed a new drain. He seemed fairly comfortable. Putting both hands on my hips I looked from one to the other of them and said, "Well?"

My patient looked at me, attempted a smile and said, "We lost four tanks." My spirits sank. Then he added, "but we got twelve and the other six surrendered." Believe me, I was catapulted to cloud nine. The sergeant continued, "I got a direct hit on the German command tank in the first five minutes. He was a lieutenant colonel. Usually we draw lots for any worthwhile effects. This time we took a vote and we unanimously decided that these should be yours." With that he opened the package on his lap. It was a Luger automatic, a pair of Zeiss military binoculars, and a 35mm Leica camera.

I was stunned and speechless. You had to be in the field with combat troops a while to realize what the gesture meant. I knew what the sergeant and his men were saying to me. They were awarding me their highest decoration, and I was deeply moved. I knew also the situation called for a gracious acceptance.

The Luger and field glasses I would always treasure. I really didn't need the 35mm camera, I had one. "Look," I finally said, "you keep the camera, I have one, and from here on in there'll be some great pictures you can get." "Yeah, but I have no film," he replied in a tone that implied he wished he did. I had a small film cartridge loader and some bulk 35mm black and white film. I reached in a drawer and gave him four fully loaded cartridges. "You do now. Get some great ones," I replied with a grin.

We broke up the mutual admiration festivities. I extracted a reaffirmation that he would continue the medication and post-op care. I also got an agreement for him to return in two days.

The next day the colonel commanding one of the regiments came back to check on casualties. He praised the tank crews for their excellent tactics and outstanding marksmanship which, he said, made the victory over the German tanks possible. When I told him of the handicap the sergeant had performed with, his jaw dropped. "I'm glad I didn't know," he said, "I might not have let him go into action."

A battlefield commission for the sergeant would have been likely earlier in the war, but not at this point. Although a medal was a certainty the colonel assured us. I was happy about the situation on several accounts, but I didn't tell him about the Luger and the binoculars.

I sent Solomon back to our parent headquarters to pick up our mail. It had been over three weeks since we had received any. He returned the next day with mail and bad news. Lou Kasman with one of the surgical teams had been killed, along with two enlisted technicians. Bayuk, the other surgeon with the team was still critical, he had taken two fifty caliber slugs in the gut.

They had been in a glider, part of an airborne crossing of the upper Rhine. The glider, clearly marked with red crosses, had been machine gunned just after landing. Lou was a good doctor and an outstanding person. He was very concerned about human suffering and human rights. So concerned, he had joined the Abraham Lincoln Brigade in Spain.

He had sought me out during training in Georgia and we had hit it off. There had been long talks on philosophy, religion, people, and the war. One day, when it was obvious we would soon be shipping out, he got quite serious. He confided his belief that he would be killed in action overseas. He raised a hand to stifle my reply. He then amazed me by asking me to pray for him when it happened. He was Jewish, I was Catholic. I promised. And then, Jew and Catholic made the commitment to pray for each other.

Lou had been gone for several weeks. I had no doubts about where he was, but if my prayers meant anything, Lou got a promotion.

My men, who frequently worked long hours, needed a break. So I took them back to one of the evacuation hospitals.

Right off the bat the commanding officer, a friend of mine, buttonholed me with a problem. The problem was a German corporal, an aidman, who had a light flesh wound. He also was, from credentials he carried, a Catholic priest. This in itself was surprising but was not the reason for the problem. The problem arose when he volunteered to say Mass for any of our personnel and wounded Germans who wanted to go to mass. The colonel asked me as a Catholic what I thought.

After thinking about it for a couple of minutes, I could not find fault with it. The church is universal as to race and color. I told the colonel this, adding that he had to approve of course. He did approve and said he'd set things up for one of the unfilled ward tents. He then asked me to be the "Master of Ceremonies."

That was fine with me and I asked to see the corporal-priest. He spoke halting English. I discovered that the good father had been on the verge of being sent to a concentration camp. He could not have used his Holy Offices there so he volunteered for the German Army as a medic. In that way he could serve his people and his God.

An hour later, the mass was announced, and a number of GI's gathered along with a few lightly wounded German POW's. I explained the circumstances to our personnel and reminded them that in a combat zone they could make their own silent confession to the Lord. They would receive conditional absolution and could then go to communion. It was well attended and the most memorable field mass I ever attended.

About midafternoon that same day, my assistant Solomon sought me out.

"Major," he said, "have you done all your business here?"

"Yeah," I responded. Why?"

His answer nearly blew me away. "Well, Lit and I are sick of the damn chicken shit of the guys here. If it's okay with you, can we go back up front where there ain't none?"

When I'd recovered from my surprise I said, "Okay, you've got it. Give me a half hour and we'll roll."

Solomon and Lit had become frustrated by the bickering and infighting at the hospital. It was unfortunate and I'm sure it was not typical of all the evacuation and field hospitals we had. Nevertheless, I went along with their wish gladly. Boy, I thought, have these guys arrived, self-confident, unselfish, and damn competent as well. I was lucky.

I could well afford to indulge the men's request. Loyalty from the top down, is an important ingredient in promoting and maintaining the kind of relationship and performance that gets things done.

Chapter 13

STARVATION CAMP

By all reports our reconnaissance units were having a field day. Suddenly one patrol radioed back shocking news. They had come upon a tent prison of about five hundred Royal Air Force officers. They were being deliberately starved to death for the sin of bombing Germany and being shot down. Many, they radioed, were in very bad shape.

Immediately the division attacked strongly and thrust a corridor through to them before they could be moved deeper into Germany. Medical officers confirmed the reports and said a great amount of medical help was urgently needed.

Two teams of physicians skilled in intravenous therapy and malnutrition were quickly culled from the groups teams and sent up the clearing station. In the meantime word had been flashed to England. In response about five hundred pints of whole blood were flown from England to an advanced air strip. Packed in ice, it was then reloaded on a large closed truck taken from some rear area outfit.

About half of the first platoon of the clearing station was to take this load of blood and the two special teams up to the unfortunate RAF men. At the last minute the clearing station commander asked me to go along, truck and all. I swung into the column and we started late in the afternoon. There was a low, heavy overcast that brought darkness rapidly.

Edwards was driving. I was beside him. We did not have a map, having run out of the map sheets we did have. However I knew the route was fairly straight. Suddenly I stiffened, something was wrong. I asked Edwards if he thought we had taken too many left turns for a fairly straight route. There was a silence for almost a minute, then he said quietly, "Damned if I don't think we have, now you mention it." We could be edging north and into enemy territory. I was worried, damn worried.

The next time the now slow moving column halted or slowed down enough I decided to hit the road and run forward to talk to the column's commander and check with him and his map.

There wasn't a chance until the column entered a small town and suddenly made a right turn down a narrow, muddy, unpaved street and halted. Running forward I groaned out loud and felt sick. The first six or seven trucks including the lead vehicle, a weapons carrier, were mired in mud up to their axles.

The overcast had, if anything, thickened. It was a very dark night. Sloshing through the mud to the weapons carrier I asked the captain why he had turned into the muddy street. Unbelievably he said a civilian he asked told him that was the best way. I winced. This was Germany not Indiana.

My flashlight lens was taped so only a thin pencil of light showed. I wanted to check his map with it. To my alarm he did not have a map, only an overlay. This is a tracing of the real map with the route indicated and two or more true map coordinates marked on it as reference points. If properly done it serves the purpose, no more than that. The one he handed me was little more than several irregular lines on paper, no reference points at all. It was useless for our purposes.

A sinking feeling filled me, I made a last try and asked for his compass. These were in very short supply for medical outfits, but as a column leader he should have had one. He didn't.

From within the town around us came voices raised in song. Nazi "fight," songs. Great! I could visualize messengers on the way to some nearby German unit telling about us. In the dark we had forfeited the protection, if any, of the red crosses.

"Look Captain," I said, "I'm relieving you and taking command, if we get out of this you can take it up with Division or Army if you want to." His voice broke as he said, "Take it, take it, I don't know what to do now."

He got down from the truck. Feeling compassion, I suggested he go sit in a truck further back in the column with some friend. With that, all the air in me came out in one agonized puff. I didn't have time to think. Quick action was imperative. To the captain's sergeant I said, "Quickly get all sergeants here, and fast." He disappeared into the blackness.

The only light was from the very small blackout lights on the vehicles about an inch and a half high. They looked like enlarged quotation marks. In this very dim light two figures materialized out of the darkness. A voice said, "Vin, take over and get us out of here." It was Major Skinner, one of the officers sent up for this mission. He was with his assistant. He now reminded me painfully that when the ice cooling the blood was melted, the blood would spoil. I told them I had taken over but getting out of here was something else again.

Edward's low voice came over my shoulder saying, "Lit's with me, want us to do anything?"

"Find out where this damn 'ditch' goes. Determine its direction, type of road surface and anything else. Watch yourselves." They took off.

Six or seven shadows were gathering around me. As they identified themselves I murmured to Major Skinner to stand by. I quickly summarized our situation and estimated we were about five miles behind enemy lines.

It was obvious the trucks, and about ten ambulances behind the mired trucks, had to be moved. Yet, the ground was quite wet. Something in the inadvertent sweep of a GI's flashlight beam caught my eye. In the meager light I saw there were some rail and picket fences nearby.

"Anyone here know what a corduroy road is?" I asked.

A voice said, "I do. We use them in logging on wet ground back home."

"Good," I said. "You're in charge. Take half the men and rip up all the fencing you need. Make us a routing around this mudhole as good as you can for the vehicles that aren't stuck. Let's go." To Major Skinner I said, "Go and encourage them, huh."

Edwards and Lit returned, sooner than I thought

they would. A narrow double lane hardtop road crossed the ditch. There was one problem. Our ditch went about fifty yards before joining the road. To the left, the road ran toward the north, I figured. To the right, it started out toward the south.

"Okay guys," I said to the three sergeants still with me, "you heard Edwards. The rest of us will help these vehicles out one at a time. Use ropes or anything else you can find. Lets go." From behind me came, "Sir, the kitchen truck is in up over its chassis. We'll never budge it."

"How long to unload it in the dark?" I asked hopefully.

Someone else said, "About three quarters of an hour."

"Too long. We'll leave it. Don't destroy it. Someone take the distributor rotor out. Hide it under the dash someplace. Our troops will pick it up in a couple of days. I doubt the Krauts will wreck it," I replied.

The first vehicle, the weapons carrier, wasn't too bad to move with all the manpower. The next five trucks taxed engines and manpower to the limit. However we got them on the macadam-like road surface. It was obvious then that the kitchen truck was there to stay, at least for a while.

The road building crew reported they were as ready as ever. The unmired vehicles pulled forward a bit. A tow line was ready to help if our corduroy road proved inadequate. Thank God, it wasn't. The credit goes to the young "logger" and his group.

All vehicles, except for the kitchen truck, were now on hardtop and ready to move. I reasoned that if the column had been edging left toward the north, a corrective route would be to the right, or south. With no map, compass, or moon or stars for orientation, I was down to sheer sense of direction.

Major Skinner offered to ride with me in the weapons carrier. "Thanks, but no," I replied. "Ride about a third of the way back in the column. If something happens to me you are in command."

With the same sergeants gathered around me as before I gave convoy instructions. There was to be no smoking or lighting of matches. Most importantly, there must be no blackout lights. They could easily be detected by troops watching the road. To compensate for this I had a man placed on the left front fender of each vehicle with his head forward. Their instructions were simple. "You can't see, but you can smell and hear the exhaust of the vehicle in front. Try and allow about a fifty foot interval. One kick on the hood means speed up, two means slow down. If things hit the fan, talk calmly. Try not to yell and draw fire. The column will not stop if fired on. Relay damage and casualty reports forward from vehicle to vehicle. Good luck."

I told Lit to drive our truck. Edwards rode on the left front of the weapons carrier which was leading off. I needed his keen hearing and eyesight. The column had to get back through enemy lines first then contact our own troops.

We moved off. Quite slowly at first. Then I found we could step up the pace to five or ten miles an hour. We crawled along at this speed for better than a half hour.

Suddenly, from the rear of the column heavy machine gun fire split the silence. Instinctively my driver slowed down. "Keep going, same speed," I said crisply. He resumed speed.

A few minutes later the report was relayed forward. "Ambulances hit, no casualties." The column kept moving. The "No blackout lights" decision had paid off. The enemy machine gunners had fired a little too high. I breathed a sigh of relief as we crossed back through the German lines.

It seemed ages later when Edwards' drumming feet on the vehicle's hood signaled for a halt. I stopped the column and joined him. He stood about ten feet in front of the weapons carrier listening intently. "Motor running, hear it?" I could hear it faintly some distance away. "I think it's in a town. The sound is bouncing off stone buildings. Hear the echo effect?" he asked.

I marveled at that deduction. "Ours or theirs?" I said thoughtfully.

"Sounds like one of our generators — constant speed."

At this point Major Skinner and two other officers materialized out of the blackness. I hastily filled them in. "What's next," said one of the officers. All along I think I knew it might come to this. Contact had to be made. It might be friend or foe, and it was my baby. "I'm going in, alone," I told them.

There was a second of dead silence. Edwards spoke first. "No. Let me go Sir, I don't count. They need you."

There was a murmur of assent. I squelched it with, "Thanks, might be okay if we knew who owned the town. We don't, so the job calls for rank."

I explained to the group that if the town was in German hands I hoped to be captured in good condition. I would then ask to be brought to the highest ranking officer. I would state the column's mission and appeal to humanitarian principles and the letter of the Geneva Convention. If there were no SS in there, it could work. Especially at this late stage in the war.

As a line officer I would have been long gone, either wounded or dead. It wasn't in my nature to ask those under me to do anything I wouldn't do. It wasn't being noble, just something inbred. So I nipped discussion in the bud and told Major Skinner he was in command. If I didn't get back in thirty minutes he was to get the column into the woods around us and not move until dawn. The red crosses on the vehicles could be seen plainly then.

They wished me luck. At the last minute good old Edwards said, "Please, I want to go with you."

"Naw, these guys need you here. This is a one-man job," I told him as I turned and started down the middle of the road.

It was then I murmured the shortest and most effective prayer of my life. It fact, it was more of an announcement than a prayer. "This is it Lord. I'm going in."

Footing on the road was good. In the almost total blackness it was not difficult to keep in the middle of the road. As I approached the town, what Edwards had detected earlier proved to be true. The sound of a running engine was echoing from the stone walls of buildings and it did sound like one of our GI generators.

My boots touched cobblestones. I was in the town. I continued to walk right up the middle of the street. I felt I had a better chance there than next to the buildings. A hand with a trench knife could stab first and its user identify the victim, me, later.

My breathing became faster and shallower as I zeroed in on the sound of what I was sure now was a generator. I went slowly. Suddenly a few yards directly in front of me there was a distinct metallic click. Simultaneously a voice in English, said, "Halt! I'll fire." Halt I did, with one foot off the cobblestones. "Major Marran, Third Army," I exclaimed in relief.

Above the generator's sound the voice came back, "Put your hands behind your neck. Take two paces forward and halt." I did. Suddenly it felt like the entire front line of the Chicago Bears hit me. My helmet flew off as I crashed down on the hard stones. One GI had hit me at the knees, another at the waist, and a third high in the chest pinning my arms. Hands went over me expertly. A low voice, almost in my ear said, "He's clean, take him to the CP."

I was helped to my feet and a man on either side chaperoned me slowly to a stone house. They then led me down steps to the cellar. They knocked on the door. After a momentary silence a voice said, "Okay." We entered into blackness. I felt the door close and an electric light came on. I was in a company command post of the 76th Infantry Division. An explosive sigh of relief burst from me.

Identification was immediate and an efficient looking sergeant apologized for the rough treatment. "We just can't take chances, Sir."

My bruises already ached. I nodded, turned to my "captors" and said, "If you have any idea of playing professional football, I'll be glad to write a letter of recommendation." The laughter broke the tension and we got down to business.

I quickly filled them in on my column and its

mission. I emphasized the urgency of getting the whole blood quickly to the RAF prisoners. They had already heard of them and their serious condition. The ranking sergeant said the platoon CO, a lieutenant, was out checking outposts, but he would give me whatever assistance he could.

On his large scale tactical map he pointed out the CP's location and the position of the RAF group. They were facing the prospect of impending combat at dawn. They could pilot us through town and point out the secured road to our objective, but that was about it.

I asked if they had another map I could use. They had none. So I asked for three minutes of silence and spent it memorizing what I had to know.

When I finished the sergeant said, "I've got a question. How in hell did you get past our two sentry posts and up to the generator?"

I was tickled and grinned. "I came in right up the middle of the street." His jaw dropped and there were several grunts from the others in the CP. He turned quickly to one of his men, "Take care of that Phil." Phil left immediately.

A corporal and I left a minute later. We made our way back to the column to find an anxious little group around the weapons carriers. Everyone was immensely relieved to find we were in friendly territory. I got the column under way. With the corporal's guidance we crawled thru the totally blacked out town. Sentries had been alerted and at the edge of the town the corporal swung down from the weapons carrier. We wished each other luck and I was on my own again.

Some time later the dim forms of several buildings

and some large tents emerged from the darkness. We had made it. GI's, shadowed by the darkness, were happy to see us. The radio net had reported us missing. As the rest of the column pulled in, officers could tell I was beat. They suggested that I sack out for a few hours. They offered to guide the column's vehicles into appropriate positions.

A GI took me into a small stone house with several mattresses on the floor. He produced a couple of GI blankets and promised I wouldn't be disturbed. I was asleep, or maybe a better description is unconscious, by the time he left the room. It was 3 o'clock in the morning.

It was about 0800 hours when I came to and sleepily made my way out onto the village street. I got about fifty feet. The clearing station CO spotted me coming and threw up his arms in mock self-protection. "Okay, Okay," he said, "I know all about it. Your two buddies swarmed all over me when I got here about dawn." He was referring to Major Skinner and his assistant.

"I'm sorry, my fault," he continued. "I didn't check to see that he had a map and compass." I just stood there and nodded. "I'm damn glad you were there. It occurred to me what high level flack there would have been if that fresh British blood had gone bad. Oh boy."

I hadn't gotten around to thinking about that. "Well, it was a rough night. How bad are these poor guys?", I asked.

"Oh God, it's not a pretty picture. Skinner and his gang are on the job. Take a look," he replied.

I walked a couple of hundred yards to the nearest of six large tents and entered. I stood there aghast.

There were rows of cots not more than two feet apart. What they held were men who had been in the prime of life when they were shot down. Merely cadaverous shadows of them remained. Major Skinner spotted me standing there and came over.

There was no comment about the night. None was necessary. "Not a nice picture," he understated. They had already arbitrarily divided the patients into three groups, roughly a third of them in each group. The worst group were very critical; starvation had progressed to the point they were little more than skeletons. They were so bad they had begun to digest their own heart muscle and would probably die no matter what was done for them.

While the next group was also skin and bones, their general condition was somewhat better, although still serious. We believed they had digested some intestinal muscle, but with blood transfusions, basic nourishment, and good care they would live. Major Skinner predicted they would need special diets, probably permanently. Their life expectancy would be shortened; the amount depended on the individual.

The last group was in fair shape. They had been more recently shot down and subjected to this brutality for a shorter period. With nourishing, readily digested food, and routine nursing care they would recover almost completely.

As Major Skinner talked, we walked slowly between the rows of British airmen. GI aidmen and medical officers passed from cot to cot. It suddenly dawned on me that the major and his team hadn't had a wink of sleep. As I was about to say something he tugged lightly on my arm. "There's someone here that wants to meet you. I told him about last night."

The man on the cot was probably in his late thirties but looked much older. He was little more than skin and bones. He was the senior ranking officer of the RAF prisoners. His rank of Wing Commander corresponded to that of Brigadier General in our Air Force.

Major Skinner introduced me. "This is the guy I told you about, Sir." The officer managed a little smile and reached for my hand. As he held it he said, "I hear you put in quite a night in getting all this help through to us. I want to thank you very much, for myself, and my fellow officers. The best of luck to you."

As I looked at him I was surprised and embarrassed. I really hadn't had time to think about it. I did know one thing. It had been worth it. I'd have done it again in a minute if the occasion called for it. The three of us chatted for a minute. Then I left.

Suddenly I was hungry. The mess sergeant got me something to eat and told me a story that shocked me to my soul. The little town's inhabitants were not unlike the monsters who had ordered the starvation of the RAF officers.

Surreptitiously, a woman resident had approached an officer. She showed him where an American pilot was buried. He had been shot down and parachuted from his fighter-bomber. So diseased were the minds of the villagers from Nazi propaganda that they tied him to a tree and stoned him to death. Shades of the Bible. It made me heartsick.

GI's had carefully exhumed his body. It was true. I decided not to ask to see it.

There was good news later in the day. The wheels

had been set in motion to fly the RAF officers right back to England. C-47 ambulance planes would take them home as soon as it was safe to move them.

Chapter 14

APOLDA

The next morning Lieutenant Gray and I hit the chow line together. He had been commanding the ambulance platoon hit by machine gun fire. We reviewed the events of the wild night. Then the subject of maps, or rather the absence of maps came up. We didn't like the situation and neither of us wanted to make a move without our own map sheets. The question was; where and how did we get them?

I had an idea. Division either did not have new sheets or didn't have enough to go around. However, we were operating in 20th Corps where I was known. They would have a supply before any of the divisions. So where was 20th Corps Headquarters? Could we get to it?

We checked with division operations. 20th Corps was moving into Weimar to the south of us and the road seemed clear. The next thing to do was get permission to go to 20th Corps and then to borrow a small weapons carrier. We set up the colonel by complaining about the lack of maps, and requesting maps we knew he didn't have. We were soon on our way in the weapons carrier after promising to get maps for the medical battalion also.

About six or seven minutes after clearing our outpost we saw a column of German soldiers. There were about a 150 of them carrying rifles, and they were coming our way. The lieutenant slowed to a crawl mumbling, "Oh my God." "Easy," I cautioned. They were wearing garrison caps, not steel helmets. This was a sign that they had no hostile intent and wanted to surrender.

As we slowed to a stop the captain leading them called out "Ich kammard." I had learned enough German to know that meant, "I surrender." With my meager German vocabulary I told him to continue in the direction we had come. In about two kilometers he would reach our outpost and they would accept surrender of him and his men. The captain nodded acknowledgement, barked an order, and off they marched.

Twenty minutes later we came to a town which I guessed had a population of ten or eleven thousand. It's name was Apolda. Its prominent feature was a good-sized railroad yard. Before we got near the yards we could see hundreds of freight cars swarming with civilians. They were looting and pillaging.

We went by as rapidly as practical and got out of there. No one seemed to notice.

We reached Weimar in about a half hour. It was a small conventional city, but picturesque. The road was deserted. As we drove into town a startling sight greeted us. German Civil Police were directing GI traffic and German pedestrians, as if there was no war. The bizarreness cleared when we saw each traffic officer being supervised by a 20th Corps MP. The

MP stood calmly on the corner as if it was all in a day's work. Finding Corps Headquarters was easy, we just pulled up and asked an MP.

Corps Headquarters was a madhouse. They were just moving in and trying to settle down. I sought out a lieutenant colonel in the MP's I knew pretty well. He would get us the maps if any were available. They had the map sheets. He reduced the number of maps I requested a little and sent his sergeant to get them.

We chatted. Then looking me straight in the eyes, he said, "Vin, I need a favor, urgently. Its about that town, Apolda." We had told him about the looting. "Among other things, there are probably munitions in some of those cars. Look," he turned to a map, "just south of town on this road is one of my lieutenants. Lieutenant Bauer. He's trained for civil affairs work and fluent in German." As he pointed to the position on the map he continued. "He's got a dozen trained men and is waiting for orders from me about the town."

We had to go back that way. The intent of his pitch was getting clearer, and I wasn't sure I liked it.

Shifting his eyes from the map he peered at me inquiringly. "It's not an order, but will you go back? Contact the lieutenant. Tell him to get into that place right away with you. Their troops have pulled out. Look around, decide what should be done and lay it on the line to the burghermeister. Be sure those civilians get out of the railroad yards."

I was simply stunned. My gut reaction was, "Why me?" Instead, I said, "But what kind of terms? By whose authority?"

"Look, Vin, I know you pretty well and I'll go

with your judgment. Decide what should be done. The lieutenant will follow through. As for authority," he continued, "you are speaking for General George S. Patton." He just looked at me, waiting.

"Okay Colonel, I'll do it. Hope to hell I don't let you down," I replied, not quite convinced I was the man for the job.

"You won't," he said with a grin as he stuck out his hand and stood up. His grip was firm; quite firm.

We started back with a roll of new map sheets. I folded the one of our area and slid it into a transparent map case. When we had put a few miles behind us I told Lieutenant Gray about my forthcoming mission. He looked at me and started to say something. Then he closed his mouth without a sound. He must have been thinking, how did I ever get into this mess?

The map was a big help and we made good time. About half a mile short of the colonel's Civil Affairs group a GI sprang out of some roadside cover and flagged us down. I noticed an M1 rifle covering us a few yards away up on a rise. There was quick identification and the GI said he'd take us to his lieutenant. The M1's stayed put.

The lieutenant and his group were holed up on a farm house on the western edge of town. I gave him the colonel's orders. He was nearly six feet tall with a confident bearing. His men obviously respected him. He liked the idea of us both going to the burghermeister's office. Before we did however, he suggested we go to the railyards and start getting people out of there.

He and I were just about to leave with his driver when he asked me if I had a gun. I was unarmed. He said I should have a gun at this stage and he would feel better if I carried one. In front of me was a table with a pile of confiscated German automatics of all kinds.

"Take your pick," he suggested.

I selected a beautifully made .32 automatic that was made by a private gunsmith in Berlin. I wondered how his boys missed it. He nodded his head approvingly and the three of us left.

The railyard itself hadn't been bombed. This puzzled me until the lieutenant explained that our air force had played it real smart. The bombers had bombed both ends of the railyard where the tracks narrowed to a couple of tracks meeting the main tracks. This precision bombing had immobilized everything in the yards and stopped mainline traffic as well.

There were three fires burning when we got to the railyard. The civilian population had grown. Most of them were milling around aimlessly. I wondered what Lieutenant Bauer planned to do. I didn't have long to wonder. As our jeep came to stop in the railyard, he stood up in the jeep. Our driver leaned on the horn and the lieutenant pointed his .45 caliber automatic skyward. Three loud reports split the air.

The milling crowd froze. It was as if a movie projectionist had stopped the projector on a single frame.

Lieutenant Bauer holstered his automatic and put his hands on his hips. I stood up in the jeep and our driver reached for his carbine and held it ready in his lap.

The motionless scene came to life and a small crowd gathered around us. It consisted of women of all ages, men over military age, and a sprinkling of young children.

Lieutenant Bauer's voice boomed out in German. "Go to your homes. Now!"

There were several replies from the people around us and a sharp exchange of German ensued. The lieutenant did most of the talking. It was unintelligible to me but I noticed a few people edging away and starting to leave. Just then a trim looking 65 to 70 year old man came up and spoke to our seated driver. I didn't catch what he said but the driver spun around. He hopped out of the jeep and said, "Come on Major, detonators and explosives!"

He and the informant took off on a run. I vaulted from the jeep's back seat and followed about three strides behind, gripping the automatic in my pocket.

About five or six tracks over the man led us to a boxcar. Two elderly men were standing guard. The boxcar's doors had been forced open. Stacked at the door were two cases of detonators used for demolition and road and land mines. Several feet away were boxcars loaded with demolition explosives.

The men were concerned that some of their townspeople would be killed or injured either by accident or the vengeful act of some diehard Nazi. They were well aware of the danger caused by the several fires in the railyard. They brought the two boxes of detonators back to the jeep with us.

Lieutenant Bauer was making little progress persuading the townspeople to leave. Sensing the opportunity, he quickly asked the three German men for their help in getting people to leave. They promptly agreed, split up, and began to circulate among the people.

We put the detonators in the jeep. Having done all we could for the present we left the railyard for the burghermeister's office. The railyard, I decided, would be number one on my agenda when we got there.

A few blocks short of the cobblestoned square one of the lieutenant's men flagged us down. He was waving a message envelope. He said a courier from 20th Corps had brought it just a few minutes ago. It reported that a company of military police, for occupation and civil administration, could not be in Apolda for at least three days. That was all. There was no comment or further instructions. Lieutenant Bauer and his dozen men would be on their own for that time. He looked at me for comment. "We'll just say that an occupational detachment will be here soon," I said.

We continued toward the town square about a half mile away. I mentally reviewed the terms I had formulated in my mind based on what I had seen of the town and its people. I felt my terms were quite humanitarian. There was no time to discuss them with the lieutenant.

As we drove into the square we were scrutinized anxiously by a scattering of civilians. A large pile of hunting and sporting rifles were stacked in front of town hall. A lone civil policeman stood guarding them. He saw us, but preferred to act as if he didn't.

Lieutenant Bauer told our driver to stay near the jeep and be visible. We decided the lieutenant would stand on my right side. He would be translating for me. I crossed my fingers briefly and dismissed the queer feeling in my stomach. Taking a deep breath I led the way up the stairs and straight ahead through double doors into the burghermeister's office.

What I saw paralyzed me for an instant. Standing facing me, twenty feet away, was a full colonel of the German Wehrmacht. Nearly six feet tall, his freshly pressed uniform was spotless. There were three or four rows of campaign ribbons above his left breast pocket and an Iron Cross at his throat. His luger's holster was slid around more than usual to the front. The black leather was so highly polished it could have been made of onyx. He wanted it to be noticed.

He was a real life example of the classic stereotype of a German Army officer. His face was impassive, but the transient suggestion of amusement glimmered there. Standing behind a long table were a captain and lieutenant. They too were armed, but not as impressive in appearance. My already tense demeanor heightened as I saw four enlisted men behind them. They were on the left seated at a bank of impressive looking military radio equipment.

I sensed Lieutenant Bauer standing stiffly at attention close to my right side. I had not expected this possibility in my worst projection. It was my move. Further procrastination would disadvantage us.

Looking into the colonel's eyes I spoke in what I hoped was a steady voice. "Colonel, I'm Major Marran from Third Army. I'm sure you realize the current military situation and its ultimate conclusion."

I paused as Lieutenant Bauer translated in a firm clear voice, then continued.

"The lieutenant and I are here to make the transition to our military government with as little difficulty and distress to your people as possible."

I paused for translation, then went on.

"First, I am concerned about the railyards. There are several potentially dangerous fires there. The presence of large numbers of civilians milling around and looting can only have unfortunate results. They should be sent to their homes."

Lieutenant Bauer's crisp translation was not even completed when the colonel turned to the radio operators and spoke rapidly.

Lieutenant Bauer, in a low voice said, "He's ordering the civil police and fire company to remove all civilians and put out any fires."

I continued, "Now, as for long term considerations. The first is food." At this point I broke off abruptly. I had noticed the colonel's expression changing as he watched my face. Before Lieutenant Bauer could translate I declared, "Colonel, you understand English pretty well I see." The colonel was taken back a bit. "Yes, Major, I do. My apologies, I should have told you at the outset."

Advantage Marran!

I asserted that we would continue in English and went back to the subject of food. I told the colonel that while we had our own supply lines, we could not supply civilian needs. The town was surrounded by farm lands. It was getting late in the season for planting food crops so it should be done immediately. I emphasized that care should be taken to check for land mines or booby traps. He nodded his understanding so I continued.

Their current food supplies should be rationed with priority given to children, the sick, and the elderly.

There was no hospital in town so I suggested a building be designated as a clinic. "If necessary," I continued, "inform the lieutenant and we will get a medical officer here for emergencies." His face brightened as he nodded. "Similarly," I went on, "it might be well to group disabled elderly together in a suitable house for better care."

"I recommend that the supply of clothing be checked, and controlled if necessary; particularly clothes for women and children."

There had long been in effect an Army General Order which put captured German Medical Supply Depots off limits. They were not to be used by Allied forces. It applied to civil medical supplies as well. The intent was that these supplies be used for the Germans.

I told the colonel to have a knowledgeable person make a list of essential pharmaceuticals and give it to Lieutenant Bauer. It would then be sent to the Corps Surgeon and the drugs supplied as soon as possible, if available. The colonel's face lit up a bit.

"Lieutenant Bauer," I went on, "has twelve German-speaking men. I see no reason why you and he can't work together using your civil police and fire brigade for our mutual benefit. Military police are coming, but I hope they won't be needed."

I paused, it was the colonel's turn. Lieutenant Bauer's feet shuffled a little. I couldn't tell if it meant approval or disapproval.

The colonel straightened, his face relaxed. "Major, your terms are both realistic and generous. On behalf of my people I accept them and will cooperate to the fullest."

I tried to disguise my sigh of relief. I felt Lieutenant Bauer relax beside me.

The colonel then explained how he had happened

to be there. He realized that the war was lost. Having grown up in the vicinity he decided to stay behind the retreating German troops and try and help his people. Two of his officers and the radio operators had elected to stay with him.

He said he would like to remain a burghermeister if possible; though he realized he and his men were really prisoners of war.

This was true of course. I told him if things worked out well in Apolda that Lieutenant Bauer and I would transmit his request giving our approval, but that the decision was out of our hands. I'm sure the colonel knew it was improbable, but he thanked me nevertheless.

It seemed a good idea at this point to have he and Lieutenant Bauer discuss immediate plans and see how they got along. I said I would leave and let them start planning, while I walked around to see if anything else needed attention.

He nodded, snapped to attention and saluted smartly. I stretched my 5'5" to it's utmost and returned his salute. It wasn't good, but as Lieutenant Bauer comforted later, it wasn't bad. I nodded to the other officers as I turned and left.

I walked around the almost deserted town square waiting anxiously for Lieutenant Bauer. A tall elderly man with a military bearing came up and handed me something wrapped in brown paper. From my poor working knowledge of German I concluded that he wanted to turn in his hunting knife. It was actually a ceremonial knife with engraved blade and ivory handle. I thanked him, saying it was superb. He nodded, turned and walked slowly away. There was undoubtedly an emotional attachment here. I almost called him back to return it. However, that would be breaking the order to turn in all knives and firearms and set a bad precedent.

In about fifteen minutes, Lieutenant Bauer came out of the town hall. He and the colonel had got along quite well. "I would have never thought of the terms you made for elderly and child care, or the idea of planting crops. I think this thing is going to work out. Let's go to the railyards and see how the police and firemen are doing. That will tell a lot."

At the railyard the police were doing a good job and people were leaving in small groups. Fires were well on the way to being extinguished. We were quite pleased and returned to the lieutenant's small command post. He immediately began briefing his men and assigning them to various duties. Lieutenant Gray and I left for Namburg after congratulatory handshakes and wishing the best for each other.

On the way back, Lieutenant Gray suggested we had put in quite a day's work for the Army. I nodded, thought a minute, then said we'd put in a good days work for both sides, and hopefully for the Good Lord.

Knowing the problem created by a lack of maps, I gave Lieutenant Gray a set and took two sets for myself. Having seen several near disasters and experiencing a near miss, I figured the extra set could come in handy. It might be needed by some outfit I'd come in contact with. The rest I gave to the colonel.

A day or two later the deep-seated hatred engendered by Nazi propaganda erupted in stark tragedy again.

The clearing station mess had been set up in the little town hall. I finished my lunch and told the two medical officers I had eaten with I had to get back. I left for the clearing station about seven or eight hundred feet away. I had gone about halfway when I heard two shots ring out.

The sound was definitely not from our rifles. I dove to the ground and looked back over my shoulder. The two medical officers I had lunched with were on the ground just a few feet from the mess building. Then in quick succession four or five other shots rang out. This time they were unquestionably GI carbines.

The two medical officers were dead. They had been shot by two German boys with their father's hunting rifles. the boys were aged twelve and thirteen. They had been immediately shot by GI military police. One lived long enough to tell the attending medic what an honor it was to die for his Fuhrer. The other died minutes later.

Chapter 15

BUCHENWALD

The irrational and unnecessary deaths of four human beings made me sick at heart. Several days later when I got orders to return to group headquarters, I was glad to go. The 76th Division was being transferred to First Army. That meant automatic detachment, since I was Third Army. Group Headquarters was much farther west. When we finally got there we were told to consider ourselves on a rest footing.

Colonel Odom had a surprise for me when I returned for one of my periodic reports. I was about to leave when he asked me to stay a few minutes. "Remember that talk we had ages ago in Normandy about pedigrees and track records?" he said. I noticed a ghost of a smile flitting across his face. He paused a moment, then went on.

"Well, Vin, you've got a track record now and a darn good one. You've become regarded as one of our better maxillo-facial men. Major Miller in one of the evacuation hospitals has got to go home. His high blood pressure is hitting the ceiling. We need someone to take over his M-F team." He hesitated for effect, "It's yours if you want it. Take a day or two to think about it if you want to."

I was surprised and a little stunned. It was the last thing I would have expected. I didn't answer for a minute. Then I answered. "Thanks Jim, but what about my men? What happens to my truck?"

"We'll get someone to take your truck of course," he paused. "Your men would have to stay with the truck. From what you and Colonel Weeks say they would be breaking in your successor."

At one point I would have jumped at the chance, but not now with the end of the war in sight. I had a smooth-running effective team. I liked them personally as well as for their work, and so did others. I wanted to be with them at the finish. "Jim," I said slowly, "if it's all right with you, my men and I would like to go all the way doing what we're doing. Thanks a hell of a lot though."

Jim chuckled, "Fine with me, I'll dig up someone." I stood up with a grin and started to leave. "Vin," he called when I was halfway to the door. I turned. "I thought you'd say that, but I had to ask. Thanks fella."

The small factory courtyard near Schluchtern where Group Headquarters was located proved to have hidden assets. Under the old, and apparently unused factory, was an underground factory extending three stories down into the earth. It had been turning out aircraft control sub-assemblies such as rudders, stabilizers, and wing control surfaces.

A couple of miles up the road was a camp for displaced persons. Late one night a man from the camp showed up, obviously quite upset. He told us there were two GI's in a jeep at the camp. "They are drunk and waving guns and trying to get some women to go with them," he sputtered.

Colonel Kind looked at me. Without batting an eye he said, "Take a jeep and three men. Get up there and get those men. Bring them back here." The last thing I ever expected to be in the war was an MP. However, there were no military police around. So now I was one.

I got my .32 automatic, picked three men from the headquarters detachment and left. One man walked ahead to watch for wires. The Germans sometimes stretched them across the road attached to demolition charges. It was a sensible precaution.

There was a minor uproar in progress when we arrived so the GI's weren't hard to find. The first sweep of my flashlight's beam showed a 20th Corps courier jeep with bags of dispatches. They were obviously destined for Third Army Headquarters. The two GI's were roaring drunk and the driver was waving a .45 automatic.

Flanked by two of my men, one with a carbine, I went up to the jeep. The GI on the passenger side of the jeep was in an alcoholic stupor, but not the driver. I yelled for his attention and identified myself. He cursed and started to swing the .45 towards me. As he did I brought my left fist down hard on his wrist. The automatic spun from his hand falling to the ground. Simultaneously I shoved my .32 automatic up in his face. It had a sobering effect. So did the carbine pointed in his direction just a few feet away. One of my other GI's held a flashlight on him.

By the time we got them back to headquarters they had begun to sober up. They now realized they were in real trouble. They had been drunk in public, and harassing people in an "off limits" displaced-persons camp. This was bad enough. Their most serious problem was that they had done all this while entrusted with classified military material.

It was now after midnight and I was ready for my sleeping bag. "No," said the colonel. A field phone call to Third Army in Frankfurt had resulted in an order to bring them in immediately.

Off I went again with the prisoners and two men in the colonel's staff car.

It was about an hour and a half drive under blackout conditions to the Military Police compound in Frankfurt. We delivered the two prisoners and I made out a detailed account of the incident and signed it. The duty officer witnessed it. With that accomplished I gladly ended a brief and distasteful military police career.

All the allied armies on the Western Front were driving east. Third Army was closing in on Regensburg. Group Headquarters, including two surgical teams and my own team, received orders to move about eighteen miles west of Regensburg. We were ready to go.

Buchenwald and Dachau, two horrible blots on humanity's history had just been discovered. They were liberated. I decided to take a short detour to see Buchenwald. I had heard that a hospital unit, several clearing companies, and a company of the Fifth Ranger Battalion were there. They were doing everything they could to help survivors.

The atrocities that were the Nazi concentration and extermination camps have been exhaustively described. Hundreds of photographs document the terrible crimes against humanity committed in these unthinkable places. I can add little to the horrors found there. They happened, they were real, and they were unimaginable.

There is, however, one thing that is seldom mentioned. It is almost impossible to convey to those who were not there. The sickening, nauseating smell.

It was caused by the odor of burned and putrefying human flesh mixed with urine and feces. It washed over me like a wave. I leaned against my truck to fight down the nausea and pull myself together. Then I turned and put my camera in a drawer of the truck. Somehow I just could not bring myself to take pictures. My mind wanted to reject the horrors of what it had seen. We bypassed Dachau.

Chapter 16

CZECHOSLOVAKIA

At the group's new location my men and I chafed at the bit. We wanted to become operational. I requested assignment to an armored division. Having worked with five infantry divisions we wanted to work with armor before hostilities ended.

Two days later the orders came. I opened them, bit my tongue, and passed the message slip to Solomon. He exploded. "Damn it, who in the hell do they think we are. Nursemaids? Those 4F's are just off the boat." Lit and Edwards echoed his lament.

The orders were to the 20th Armored Division, just arrived from the United States. I was angry too though less vocal. There had to have been a mistake, but orders were orders. I checked for the 20th's location and we departed. Later I'd ask questions.

We had gone six or seven miles. Edwards, who was driving, expressed his disappointment by driving too fast. I didn't have the heart to slow him down just then. We heard an automobile horn honking from behind. It was persistent and Edwards slowed down some. He said, looking in the rear view mirror, that the driver of a staff car was motioning us to the side of the road. "Better stop," I said. "Pull over." He did, as I thought, What now; speeding?

We pulled over and stopped. The staff car screeched to a halt just ahead of us. Colonel Weeks jumped out and came back yelling, "I'm sorry, it was a mistake!"

He went on to explain he had not been at headquarters when the order was given. It was issued by a young new captain that he was breaking in. On his return he found out and thought, "Oh my God, they'll hate me." He had taken off after us to personally rescind the order.

"How does the Fourth Armored sound to you guys?" he asked. The Fourth Armored was a great armored division indeed. In fact, the Fourth Armored was to General Patton what the Tenth Legion was to Julius Caesar. This was more like it; the ultimate. They were driving east and we'd be in at the finish. The Colonel shook hands with each of the guys thanking them for a "great job." Then he jokingly asked, "Am I forgiven?"

We assured him he was. He told us to get the division's location at 20th Corps Headquarters now in Regensburg. A quick check on the map for roads and we took off.

We found the Fourth Armored in wooded hills northeast of Regensburg. They were ready to knife into Czechoslovakia in what was probably the last such drive of the war in Europe. The division surgeon sent us to Combat Command B, commanded by Colonel Sears. He gave us a warm welcome.

An almost instant flood of business hit us. The division had been so mobile personnel hadn't had the chance for anything but emergency care for some time.

On the second day a very amusing episode took place. Way back at Fort Adams on Narraganset Bay, I had an excellent dental assistant named Priest. I had no idea then he was a medic in the Fourth Armored. I was working on an officer when a GI burst into the truck bellowing, "Hello, you old son of a bitch! Haven't they killed you yet?"

Everyone froze. I recognized him instantly. "You dirty bastard, did the whole goddamn firing squad miss?," I quipped back. Whereupon the two of us wrapped our arms around each other. The stunned spectators just looked at each other. We quickly explained our friendship before someone called the military police and had us put away. It was good to see him. I found out he was considered a darn good medic, which is what I would have expected.

Priest's immediate CO took me on a tour of the command's aid stations explaining how they work with armor in combat. At one, I found out something about their discipline. It was one of the things that made the division so good.

I was talking to two medical officers. They were set up in an aid station that was little more than a shack. Two GI's hustled in a third GI bleeding from a cut in the forehead. He had obviously been drinking. They were angry with him. The two enlisted medics showed some anger as well as they plunked him down on a stool.

The medical officers didn't budge as the aidmen cleaned up the wound in the GI's forehead. It needed a couple of sutures. To my amazement they began to suture it without local anesthesia. The GI flinched and started to slip off the stool. They let him. As they roughly hauled him up on the stool again, one of them belted him open-handed across the face. "Sit still you bastard," roared one of the sergeants who had brought him in.

At this point I couldn't take it anymore and said to the medical officers, "What the hell is this? Tell me!"

"Everything's under control," said one calmly. "Jack, will you explain to the major." Jack was the sergeant who had brought in the injured GI.

"Well, Sir," said Jack, "as you know, our tanks aren't quite as good as Jerry's. We make up for it by better maneuvering and better gunnery. We are on alert to attack and this bastard hit the bottle. He knows better. He's a gunner and his drinking has made his tank a casualty. Now do you understand?"

"Understood," I nodded.

The GI continued to get rough treatment. "You know," said one of the medical officers bemusedly, "Those guys are pretty good at suturing. They've sure had one hell of an internship."

That evening during chow the orders came from division headquarters. Combat Command B's line of attack led east straight through Strakonitz, Czechoslovakia, and then hooked northeast toward Prague. Combat Command A was the north arm of a pincer movement on Prague. "We move out at 0600," said Colonel Sears. Then he turned to me, "Ordinarily I'd send you back to division, but I don't expect much resistance. If you'd like to come along, you're welcome."

Would I like to go along? Damn right I would, and

I said so. He grinned.

At dawn the next day the sound of engines vibrated the air and the lead unit moved out. We followed along with an armored medical section. I heard raucous cheers as we neared the frontlines. Then we were laughing too. At the side of the road, nailed to a tree, was a two foot by four foot sign. It proudly proclaimed, "You are now entering Czechoslovakia through the courtesy of the Fifth Infantry Division."

Before evening we entered Strakonitz, and the outposts went a few miles further east. It was a pleasant Czech town. The welcome was impressive. The townspeople turned out waving Czech flags and an occasional American one. The orders were to sit tight and wait for further orders. Nobody liked to wait. Prague was only about seventy miles away; two days drive, perhaps less.

The medics suddenly became busy. Not with GI's, but beaten and wounded collaborators who were now fair game for the people. There were even several communist agents. Some of the beatings were severe enough to be fatal.

A firearms plant in the town had been turning out automatic pistols for the Russians. The Czechs were so happy about their liberation that they offered to make a deluxe 7.65 caliber automatic for each of our officers. The offer contained an interesting feature. Each officer would be given an appointment. At that time he could move along the manufacturing line watching the pistol being made. He could observe it from the first fillets of metal to the finished gun, including testing and firing. Then he could fire the new gun he had seen made for him.

I was fascinated by the manufacture of my gun. A town shoemaker actually beamed in gratitude when I asked him to make a holster for it. I'm a southpaw and he made a nice right shoulder holster for me.

The combat troops chomped at the bit. The Prague underground had captured the radio station and pleaded with us to come. Unseen summit decisions made by the high command called the shots. Allied western front armies were to go only so far they said. Then wait for the Russian troops to come from the east. It wasn't easy and the townspeople didn't understand. They confided that they feared the Russians and hoped we would not withdraw.

Chapter 17

THE RUSSIANS ARRIVE

The Russians were still several days march away. An uneasiness permeated the air.

Finally, about noon one day, a unit of Malenovsky's First Ukrainian Army showed up. There was an immediate confrontation.

They said we Americans didn't know how to handle conquered territory. So their general said he was going through us for about another twenty miles. The command's troops to a man said, no. General Hoge, the division's commander, called for a conference with the Russian commander.

The medical station had been set up in a town clinic. Just before the meeting to the east of town, he came to see us. His problem was real. He explained that at the meeting the Russian general would immediately uncork 150 proof vodka and pour it into water glasses. He would then offer toasts, to everything imaginable. The Russians would consider it an insult not to drink with them. Furthermore, they would attempt to outdrink the Americans and believed they would humiliate us if they were successful.

"I don't drink much anyway. How do I keep from passing out cold?" he queried.

It sounded funny at first, but then quite serious. His status and credibility as a negotiator was in jeopardy. Medics, both enlisted and officers, put their heads together and came up with a prescription. The general was given eight to ten ounces of medically pure mineral oil to drink. Then someone rounded up a fresh-baked loaf of Czech bread. The alcohol would dissolve readily in the mineral oil and pass on through the intestines. The fresh spongy bread, eaten without the crust, would soak up the vodka and significantly delay its absorption.

It worked. Some of us went forward to watch the conference. I took a photograph showing General Hoge leaning nonchalantly against his jeep with a water glass half-full of straight vodka in his hand. His Russian counterpart stood flanked by a couple of officers, all with glasses of vodka of unknown strength. We suspected they weren't as strong as what they were serving the Americans.

The conference, apparently unknown by the Russians, was being broadcast all over the combat command. While they were talking General Hoge's driver sat in the jeep with his thumb depressing the transmit button on the radio. Every radio equipped vehicle, and every unit, including medical units, were listening. General Hoge's comments for the benefit of the division's listeners were informative and occasionally caustic.

Along the tree-lined road American and Russian

GI's were mingling in a friendly fashion. Languages like German, Polish, and Lithuanian, as well as Russian and English were channels of communication.

I found a Russian medical officer, a captain, and his assistant, a young lady lieutenant. I spoke no Russian, but they both spoke fairly good English. We got along fine. Among other professional topics, we discussed primary aid to the wounded.

A reconnaissance unit of the Fourth Armored had liberated a Russian pilot some time ago. He had been shot down over Germany and had hidden. Actually, he was a Lithuanian who had been a salesman and knew Germany very well. Rather than be repatriated, he offered to join the reconnaissance outfit where he would be very valuable.

The Fourth winked a little at repatriation procedures and welcomed him with open arms. On this day he was verbalizing quite loudly to a group of Russian GI's on what a great bunch the Americans were and what fine fighters they were as well.

Suddenly, out of the corner of my eye, I spotted a rather angry looking Russian major bearing down on the group. My new friend, the captain, noticed and looked grim. "Political commissar," he murmured in English. The commissar had spotted the loquacious speaker and realized that he had defected. He angrily broke up the group. The adopted Russian had ducked in alarm.

Sensing more trouble, I excused myself and went after him. I found him huddled with two of his recon buddies. The commissar was looking too, so I shepherded him over to a chaplain who, fortunately, was nearby with his jeep. I asked him to take off and get him back to the division headquarters where they could give him protection.

When the jeep was well on its way up the road, I turned and found the air of conviviality had been broken. The Russian GI's were being herded away from our men. The Americans felt bad about it. There was a very thoughtful look on the face of my friend the captain and his young female assistant. Seizing the moment, I said to the captain, "What are your thoughts?"

He looked at me with an unhappy, resigned look and answered prophetically. "You know, your country and mine are destined to rule the world for the next few centuries. If we can't talk to each other and become friends, it will be a rough future." I nodded in agreement and we talked for another ten minutes or so.

I arose, shook hands with him and the young lady, and explained that I had to get back to my station so some other medical officers could come up in turn.

Many, many, times over the years since World War II, that meeting and that conversation has sprung back into my mind. How prophetic it was. I always wonder if there was something we, the United States and our British and French allies, could have done then to keep the ice from getting so thick and impenetrable.

From eavesdropping on General Hoge's conversation with the Russian commander it was obvious that things were not going well at that level either. The Russian general continued insisting he would pass through us for about twenty miles because we didn't know how to handle "conquered" people.

This had been going on for over two hours and General Hoge's patience had understandably worn thin. He reached over and took the jeep's radio mike and spoke crisply. "To Combat Command B. We've tried. Apparently these guys only understand one kind of language, force. Command, clear for action; attack formation."

Immediately the relaxed air of the command vanished. Unit orders filled the radio channels. Tanks, light armor, and the command's artillery moved into position. Our treatment station became less of a clinic and more like a casualty reception station.

Then, with the mike still open, General Hoge turned to his Russian counterpart. "I think you'll find we do know how to control an occupied area. You can take your jeep and two other officers and drive into Strakonitz and see for yourself." Incidentally, the jeep was lendlease from the United States, but the Russians thought they were made somewhere in the Ural Mountains.

The people in the town, sensing trouble, became alarmed; but were reassured by our officers and GI's. Sure enough the Russian commander and two of his officers came into town in their jeep. The main street was crowded with townspeople. The attack formation of the command spoke very loudly. It was an interesting spectacle. Without a word they drove back to where General Hoge was waiting and conceded our ability to control the area.

At this point General Hoge reminded them they had already advanced several miles beyond the line agreed on at Yalta. The Russian CO acknowledged this and asked that he and his troops be allowed to bivouac there for the night. He said they would drop back to the agreed on phase line in the morning. Third Army Headquarters had been kept informed and authorized the Russian request. General Hoge came back into town and the command relaxed a little. The combat formation, however, remained.

Meanwhile, this information was being sent back to Third Army and from there to SHAEF, Supreme Headquarters Allied Expeditionary Forces. That was where, in our judgment, a fairly serious mistake was made. Possibly, representations were made by the Russian high command regarding occupation in the Strakonitz area. In any event, word came down the chain of command to Army and on to Division that the Russian troops were to be allowed to stay where they were. They were permitted to stay there until further Russian-American conferences were held, phase line notwithstanding. An on-the-scene appraisal would, we felt, have dictated otherwise. As the world now knows, they never left.

In retrospect, the cardinal sin was in allowing an exception to the Yalta phase line agreements. It was a crack that became a chasm. The flexibility of the western allies telegraphed to the Russians that if they pushed hard enough, we would bend. To them, it looked like weakness.

Tension between forces remained high. It increased when a drunken Russian major tried to cross a small bridge guarded by two of our GI's. One of the GI's, carbine held diagonally across his chest so as to not be provocative, said the major could not pass. The major's angry response was to reach for his holstered automatic. From fifteen feet away, the other GI fired his carbine from the hip and hit the major in the chest.

In our treatment station, we found the wound was very serious. We felt he should not be moved until, and if, he improved. Two Russian officers, one a medical officer showed up the next morning. They had to be dissuaded from immediately taking him back to their lines. Told the move might kill him, the line officer said it wouldn't make much difference. He claimed he would probably be shot anyway for being drunk and causing trouble with the Americans.

The Russians took him away in an ambulance in about a week, after he had improved.

Then it arrived, VE-Day.

For some of us it was anticlimactic. Third Army, First Army, and the British had all met and linked up with the Russian Army at several points. Surprisingly at first, the Czechs greeted the news with decided uneasiness. The first anxious question was whether or not we would pull back and leave them to the Russians. This question was immediately followed by, "If you do pull back — when, and how far?"

We tried to reassure them without making definite statements. We just didn't know. In fact, had we known what happened at Yalta, we would have been unhappy and embarrassed. All through the ranks we were frustrated that we had not been allowed to go on to Prague, just seventy miles away.

One tank gunner said to me, "Let's get this damn thing over, now. I don't want to see my sons coming back some day to finish the job."

Townspeople told us that a day or two before we had arrived, Communist agents had begun revealing themselves. They had discouraged any display of American flags or enthusiastic welcome. In a house-to-house campaign they offered people Russian flags to display. They suggested it would be a good idea, since they would end up controlled by the Russians.

They even took down the names of those who refused them. They ended up with a long list. There were few takers.

Unexpectedly the treatment station had four local civilian casualties. They were very badly beaten up local Communist agents who had surfaced. One of them died. A local Czech physician and one of the medical officers had become friendly. He appeared one day wearing the uniform of a captain in the now non-existent Czech Army. What he told our medical officers was startling.

During several late evening bull sessions in the treatment station, he gave us an outline of the history of eastern Europe. He went on to forecast the more immediate future of the area. He described the piece by piece engulfment of the Baltic States, Poland, Czechoslovakia, and Hungary by Soviet Russia over a period of a few years. Austria, he felt was a big "maybe."

We were impressed, the doubters among us couldn't believe that the United States and Britain would allow it. The captain's reply was simply, "How will you prevent it? Will you be ready to use force of arms?" Then he reminded us that the war in the Pacific was not yet over by any means.

I was one of those who were convinced. Convinced enough that I wrote the timetable of engulfment he prophesied home in a letter to my mother, a history buff. She kept all my letters. About the time of Winston Churchill's "Iron Curtain" speech, she brought it out and read it with me. I gasped! The Czech doctor's takeover timetable had been accurate to within a few months.

The Russian high command gave permission to

parade a company of infantry into Strakonitz and back. It was difficult to swallow. The parade, such as it was, had no band music and more curious GI onlookers than townspeople. Even though the Russians wore no helmets and their rifles were unloaded, it was a bit difficult to swallow.

With mixed feelings, about a week later, the Fourth Armored received orders to withdraw from Czechoslovakia. My team and I went with Combat Command B to the area of Kelheim on the Danube River. Kelheim is a quaint little town set on an island. The command's medics set up in the town square.

At this time, the war with Japan was in full swing. Top staff officers were being rotated home for leave with the prospect of reassignment to the Pacific Theater. Colonel Weeks and Colonel Odom left with brief goodbyes and were replaced by officers fresh from the United States.

Tremendous news came with our mail. There was a note from Colonel Kind that sent the whole surgical group into ecstatic celebration on cloud nine. The group had been awarded the Meritorious Service Plaque by order of General Patton.

This not too well known unit citation originated with General George Washington at Valley Forge. It was intended to recognize units of his army that had shown continuously high performance over time. It served also to recognize those units that had stuck it out during that long winter at Valley Forge. It can only be awarded by the commanding general in the field.

All personnel of the unit cited, officers and men alike, wear an embroidered wreath of oak leaves about three and a half inches in diameter just above the cuff on the right sleeve. The group's officers were delighted to see the enlisted medics given the recognition they richly deserved.

The group's citation read, in part, "For sustained superior performance during the European campaign of the United States Third Army."

A Bronze Star for a medical officer for his performance was fine. No one turned it down, but the fact remained that his performance depended in large measure on the backup assispance he received from his enlisted technicians and nurses. The same was true for the anesthetists of course.

The smiles on my men's faces when they received the patches to sew on their sleeves were heart warming. They sewed on the patches the first chance they had and made certain their buddies in the clearing station saw and heard all about it. I'm sure this scene was repeated in all of the group's teams.

Chapter 18

SALZBURG

It was a little surprising when my men and I received orders assigning us to Fifth Army Headquarters in Salzburg, Austria. However, the Salzburg area was beautiful. If we were not to go home for a while, this was welcome duty. When I saw the area, I had to admit my beloved White Mountains had met their match.

We set up in the middle of Salzburg, outside a building where the headquarters dental officers had set up a dental clinic.

We centered our efforts on prosthetic dentistry, such as dentures and removable partials and bridges. As before, we did no fillings. The clinic's dental officers handled those.

We'd been there about a week when I did some work on the captain commanding the headquarters detachment. We became quite friendly and he asked me to join him for dinner at their officer's mess. It was in the hotel's old dining room. The captain had procured a little private room in a corner for himself and a few close friends. It held eight people, booth style.

Our little group loved it. It was the scene of many discussions that continued for hours. We discussed Japan and the Pacific area, but mainly Germany, Soviet Russia, and the future of Europe.

"The Bomb" and Japan's surrender came suddenly. It was a bewildering almost intoxicating surprise, followed by reflection and thankfulness.

Johnny, my friend the captain, supervised the motor pool as well. He came up with an old Mercedes convertible which he placed at my disposal in the headquarters motor pool. The clinic had twenty-four hour emergency coverage of course, but routine clinic hours were eight to four-thirty weekdays, and noon on Saturday.

Having a car was a wonderful opportunity. Late afternoon and week-end excursions to the picturesque Tyrolean mountains and lakes, such as Wolfgangsee and Halstadt were a joy. Particularly after the hell of months of combat.

Officers were quartered in an old hotel near the mess and clinic. We got maid service by chipping in to pay two young Polish girls. They had escaped from Poland ahead of the Russian sweep and got down to Austria via an underground railway escape route. The fare, unfortunately, was paid by sleeping with half a dozen German officers along the way. At least the two girls were unharmed and healthy. The younger of the two was in her early twenty's. She was blonde, had a slight figure, and very pleasant personality. She had been about halfway through a Polish university when war broke out. Her name was Katherine.

Maria, the older and prettier of the two, had a degree in music. Surprisingly, she had a degree in electrical engineering as well. When we found that she was an accomplished pianist a good piano was found. The hour of beautiful music almost every evening after dinner will be remembered fondly by most of us.

Both could use more money but firmly declined charity. So we suggested that they help wait on tables in the officer's mess, along with several local Austrian young ladies. They jumped at the offer and then accepted our financial assistance. With this, and money from their maid duties, they promptly bought some nice clothes and had their hair done. The resulting transformation was darn near breath-taking.

A few days later at lunch, the lieutenant colonel commanding the area's medical personnel, brought an Austrian physician to lunch. He introduced him to all of us. He was from the Wolfgangsee area and they were meeting to coordinate military and civil medical services.

Maria came out of the kitchen with a tray of luncheon plates. She started toward the table where they were sitting. I was looking at her and saw her freeze as an expression of fear and horror swept over her face. She trembled, and a plate slipped from the shaking tray. She recovered enough to put the tray down on the nearest table, shielded her face with one hand, and fled back into the kitchen. It had happened fast and few besides myself had noticed.

I got up hastily and went into the kitchen where I found Maria and her friend Katherine in each other's arms, crying. Several Austrian girls were chattering in German, alarmed but not knowing what to be alarmed about. I went to Maria and disentangled her from Katherine. I sat her down on a convenient bench and asked her to please tell me why she and Katherine were so alarmed. I was sure it had something to do with the civilian physician.

The mess sergeant used his head and started the paralyzed kitchen force serving per usual. I herded Katherine and Maria out a back door and into a quiet corner of a nearby building. "Maria, the sight of the doctor completely upset you; and Katherine too when you told her he was there. You must tell me why; now."

Maria finally got control of herself and her story came out disjointedly, primed by my occasional questions. The Austrian doctor, was not what he seemed to be. Maria acknowledged he was a doctor, but not an Austrian doctor. In fact, she insisted he was a member of the Nazi Party and had been active in the Nazi sterilization program. Katherine corroborated her story.

The girls ran into him during their escape from Poland. He forced them to submit to degrading and unnatural physical acts at his hands. He tried to keep them by threatening their lives if they did not stay. Courageously, they escaped anyway in the middle of the night and got through to Salzburg. Now, seeing him hand in glove with American medical officers, they understandably feared the worst.

I took some time to get their story clear in my mind. I then asked Maria, the more articulate of the two, if she would come with me to the local Army Intelligence Section. I wanted her to repeat the entire story, including the part about leaving Poland. I explained there would be a lot of questions. The intelligence officer needed to get all the information he could. I was pretty sure the doctor would be arrested by our military police and they wouldn't have to worry about him again.

Maria agreed. The session at intelligence lasted about an hour and a half. The young captain we spoke with had a working knowledge of Polish and made it as easy for Maria as he could. It turned out the doctor was indeed a German Nazi. He was in the "Automatic arrest category." This consisted of people already considered guilty of war crimes and atrocities. They were to be arrested on sight.

We didn't see the doctor again and the girls soon returned to normal. Maria and I became good friends resulting in some very enjoyable and substantive talks together. She was looking forward to returning to post-war Poland and using her electrical engineering knowledge to help rebuild it.

I've often wondered what happened to Maria and Katherine. I hope they both stayed in Austria and found nice young men.

My technicians were naturally friendly. They had little difficulty socializing. This was especially true after Army Special Services and the U.S.O. set up an activities and social center in Salzburg. I did some dental work for a sergeant on the staff one day and we became friendly. He asked me if I was interested in going down to Gross Glockner, the glacier in the Tyrol. We could stay a couple of nights in one of the small mountain hotels and do some skiing.

I jumped at the chance, especially when he said that two of my men could go along. Edwards hated snow, which made it easy for me. I didn't have to choose which two went. So the sergeant said he'd get a guide, dig up a jeep (the Mercedes wouldn't do the job), and get back to me. I got permission from the local medical command.

A couple of days later I got a note saying we were set for the next day. The note also suggested we stop and see Hitler's Berchtesgaden on the way. Officers could go up to Hitler's mountaintop retreat known as the "Eagle's Nest."

Chapter 19

BERCHTESGADEN

Bright and early Goldberg, Litiborski, and I arrived at the Special Services Center to check in, pick up our jeep, and a guide. Things seemed busy.

As I was wondering who I should ask for help, someone tapped me on the shoulder. I spun around to find myself looking into the eyes of a very attractive Austrian girl with an amused smile. "Are you Major Marran?" said the lovely voice with just a trace of an Austrian accent. "Yes," I replied. "My men are checking out a jeep and I'm looking for our guide."

"That's me. I'm your guide," she smiled. "There's my gear over in the corner." Her pretty head motioned the direction. Speechless I strolled over to the corner and found her gear. I recovered enough to say, "Gee, what a nice surprise." We went out in the parking lot where Goldberg and Litiborsky were checking out the jeep. When they spotted the young lady and me they smirked and gave knowing glances to each other. "Mickey," as she introduced herself, had us all mesmerized.

On the road and out of Salzburg, Mickey, sitting in the front with me as I drove, told us her last name was Pembrauer. She asked where in the "States" I came from. "Well," I said, "you probably won't recognize the name but it's a moderate-sized city about ninety miles west of Boston. It's called Springfield."

"Springfield," she exclaimed, "I know it well! There's Steiger's, Forbes and Wallace, the Highland Hotel; and Wayside, the nice restaurant between Springfield and Holyoke." It's a wonder the jeep didn't zigzag all over the road. I was dumbfounded. She had named the two largest department stores, the main hotel, and my favorite restaurant. Goldberg and Litiborski were leaning forward with great big ears. "Okay. I give up," I said while she roared with laughter. The rest of the way to Berchtesgaden she told me her story.

She had been captain of the last Austrian Women's Olympic Ski Team before Hitler took over the country. At the winter Olympic games, she was approached by the athletic director of Smith College in Northampton, Massachusetts (about 18 miles north of Springfield). He invited her to go to Smith as a skating and ski instructor. She accepted and soon was invited by the Smith girls to homes, parties, football games, and the theater.

After several years the clouds of war began to form over Europe. She decided to go home to see her parents. While she was home, Hitler moved into Austria and she was trapped. Having a fine personality and being an outstanding athlete, she had many friends. She told them about life in American and about its people.

I still chuckle today at the illustration she used to counter the Nazi assertions that Americans were unwilling and unable to fight. Smith girls had "fixed her up" with male escorts and she had seen a number of football games, mostly Ivy League. Watching games in the late fall really impressed her. The New England weather can be so capricious.

Mickey had painted a word picture to them of football. Twenty-two young men, eleven on each side. Pushing, running, throwing, or kicking an oval-shaped ball to the end of a one hundred yard field. All of this in two to four inches of mud and near-freezing weather. Their uniforms, she added, were unrecognizable in about five minutes.

There had been one game, she remembered, that was played in a couple of inches of snow. A snow squall had made it difficult to see the players. Mickey's conclusion was simple. "Give these young men guns and get them angry. Then look out. They'll be tough. Given the provocation, America will fight."

Mickey's troubles started when the Gestapo heard about her stories. After a background check, they decided she must be an American agent. Tipped off, Mickey had taken to the mountains with a backpack and her mountain skis. She went from hamlet to hamlet and mountain hut to mountain hut. Sometimes she was only a day or two ahead of the German mountain patrols looking for her. This went on nearly four years until the Germans lost her track. Eventually, when our armies knifed into Austria, she came down out of the mountains and identified herself to the Americans. She ended up working for our Special

Services and U.S.O. group.

Later, I learned she had done more than just run, there had been some hit-and-run as well. Mickey Pembrauer had helped to organize some mountain resistance groups and on occasion she participated in ambushing German mountain patrols.

The town of Berchtesgaden was a picturesque Tyrolean town set in a valley. From Berchtesgaden a well-graded hardtopped road wound up a mountainside. It stopped about one thousand feet short of the top of the mountain, overlooking the valley. At the end of the road was a parking area almost full of GI vehicles.

Mickey and my men were not permitted to go further. I went on. I was directed to an imposing tunnel entrance set into the rocky side of the mountain. Two huge, heavy, wooden doors studded with bronze bolts were partly open. Entering, I saw a concrete tunnel, twelve to fourteen feet wide. It led several hundred yards deep into the mountain. At the far end of the tunnel was a pair of shining brass elevator doors emblazoned with the German Imperial Eagle and the Nazi swastika.

In an elevator which would have done credit to the Waldorf Astoria's ballroom elevators, I rode up through the mountain. At the top the elevator doors opened noiselessly to a lush and spacious mountain chalet. I stepped from the elevator into a wide foyer studded with brass Nazi symbols and the German Eagle. Opposite the elevator was a large, narrow white and gold table. A huge wall mirror extended from the marble table top to the ceiling.

Back under the mountain top was a fully-equipped

kitchen. It had every modern convenience for that time. There were numerous bedrooms, including Hitler's private suite. Unfortunately time did not permit me to view them.

Returning to the foyer I stepped up to a balcony furnished similarly. It looked over a huge, semicircular room. It was about four feet below the balcony and reached by two sets of steps on either end. The room had a wall of glass framing a breathtaking view of the Tyrolean mountains. I was captivated by the view of such awesome beauty.

After several minutes of hypnotic fascination, I surveyed the room itself. Several massive, leather-upholstered sofas were arranged following the semicircle of the room. Attractive cocktail tables served the seating areas. Large, comfortable, occasional chairs were scattered about; each with its own end table. It was a scene of majestic, baronial splendor.

This was Hitler's "Eagle's Nest," the scene where Hitler planned many of his tactics. Closing my eyes, I could picture Mussolini with Borman, Goering, Goebbels, and other high-ranked Nazi personalities sitting engrossed by Hitler's oratory.

This magnificent edifice was later destroyed to prevent it from becoming a shrine to Nazi fanatics. In retrospect, it was a shame to blow up the entire installation. One does not erase history by destroying its artifacts.

Back down in the parking lot I noticed a small group of plain single-story buildings nestled off to one side. What drew my attention to them was the presence of several American Military Police guards. A military police captain was coming my direction. I stopped him and asked what the buildings were. "Do you know what the bastards were doing there?" he answered. "They were experimenting, trying to find ways to decrease the gestation time in animals. Then they planned to try and apply it to humans! More cannon fodder quicker for the Reich, eh?"

We drove down the mountain into the valley again and on south. Then we began the climb to Gross Glockner. We arrived in the late afternoon at a small mountain lodge full to the brim with GI's. The food was terrific and in the thinner air of that altitude, sleep came early and easily.

As the sun arose the next morning, the place came to life. There were no late sleepers. After Mickey had outfitted me with skis, she led me out to the glacial snow. Goldberg and Litiborski took one look and begged off, after silently letting me know with whom they figured I had spent the night.

I had been only an occasional weekend skier at home. Standing on glacial snows at eleven thousand feet with an Olympic skier, I prepared myself to be humiliated. It turned out to be not quite that bad. Mickey gave me an exceptionally good lesson, and I was a most willing student. On a scale of one to ten, I judged my efforts to be about four and a half. Mickey said eight.

I asked Mickey to demonstrate her Olympic style. The exhibition was a symphony of grace, flowing movement, and incredible power, just when it was needed. It left me in awe, and grinning with admiration. There were a couple of more days out on the glacier. I improved, somewhat. I discovered the need to limit physical exertion in the thin air. Mickey thrived on it.

Neither Goldberg nor Litiborsky had ever skied, but both gave it a try. They said they wished they had tried it years before. The first thing they did was immediately sit down and write home about their experience. Then it was down from the sublime and back to the realistic. We took a different route back to Salzburg. It was a beautiful ride.

About a week later, Mickey invited me to a dinner party. The Austrian men and women working with Special Services and the U.S.O. were giving it for the American officers in Salzburg. It was in the cabaret style, complete with floor show. My friend Mickey decided to liven things up a bit, and surprise me in the bargain.

There was a beautiful chorus line of about a dozen dancers. They were doing a creditable job for the hastily arranged affair. Suddenly, one of them broke ranks and made a beeline for me. She sat down on my lap, threw her arms around me, and before I knew it we were cheek to cheek. The entire room erupted in waves of laughter. When I managed to get a look at Mickey she was reveling in the success of her coup.

With Mickey's intimate knowledge of the country, and the good old Mercedes, we got to many out-of-the-way places on weekends. Sometimes when she was working, I'd take Edwards, Solomon, and Litiborski to some of the places she'd shown me. Areas they would not otherwise have seen. At the same time we were eagerly awaiting orders which would start us on the way home.

Mickey and I faced the growing realization we were fond of each other. We talked it out. Had I not been spoken for and had a family I dearly wanted to see I would have tried to stay there and bring her home with me. I had it on good authority she would have come.

Then in the fall, around October, the orders came. They had been kicked around in several headquarters greatly complicating my schedule. As a single officer, I had to be attached to a homeward-bound unit. The result was that I finally sailed for home six or seven weeks later than the orders originally had intended.

Shakespeare said that "parting is such sweet sorrow." Yet I don't believe even the Bard felt the complexity of emotions I felt leaving Salzburg. Mickey, the beautiful country, and feelings of love and longing for home, wife, children, and parents.

Edwards shut down our generator and secured the trailer to the truck's hitch for the last time, at least for me. We rolled out of Austria headed for Bavaria — my mind once again a kaleidoscope of images. We had been part of a historic war.

It wasn't easy leaving my men when we turned in the truck and its equipment. We had been a team in every sense of the word. If I looked good, and perchance at times, very good, their backup and initiative made it so. Edwards, Solomon and Litiborski, All-Americans.

Chapter 20

HOMEWARD BOUND

Finally, after some miscues, I reached the big sprawling embarkation camp outside of Marseilles. From its appearance it was a disorganized mess. The Army had devised a point system to determine priorties for going home. It had its virtues, but it also had its vices, as I soon found out.

The general hospital unit I ended up with had all kinds of people attached as a vehicle for getting shipped home. Tankmen, infantrymen, truckers, bakers, and many others were in it. Unit identity was lost. The transportation people did not understand the pressure built up in the minds of veterans who had spent long months in combat. These men simply wanted out; to go home. They had little patience with the logistical problems delaying their departure.

It erupted one day. A hospital unit, now a vehicle for combat men, boarded a ship in the harbor of Marseilles. When the group was all on board, it dawned on some well-meaning transport officer there were neither separate nor what he called appropriate toilet facilities for the nurses. There were approximately twenty-five still attached to the unit. With myopic mentality he decided to turn around and disembark the entire unit of about five hundred personnel. He wanted to wait for a boat suitable for the nurses you see.

The combat veterans did not see! En masse, they went to the rail of the boat and dumped their duffle bags over the side into the foul harbor water. "Inexcusable and mutinous," declared the port authorities. "They should all be court-martialed. Draw up charges."

I was conscripted into the mess. A chaplain I had become friendly with came to me with the story. He asked if I would help with suggestions and talk to the rebel group's self-styled leaders. They were all decorated combat veterans, and all sergeants. His idea was to mitigate the situation and see if there was some way to get them back on a shipping list, soon.

The padre and I arranged a conference with the four sergeants representing the several hundred men. I shined up my oak leaf insignia a little and made sure the five battle stars on my European Theater ribbon were nice and straight.

The four sergeants were spotless and erect. Each had an impressive array of ribbons and decorations. There were three or four battle stars, purple hearts, Bronze Stars, and Silver Stars. One man sported a Distinguished Service Cross. I was intrigued and felt a kinship when I saw one of the men wearing the blue and silver Combat Medic medallion.

The Combat Medic decoration was an impressive medallion about one and one eighth inches high by about two inches long. It depicted a silver litter on a field of blue, surrounded by an oval wreath of silver. It meant that the sergeant had treated many wounded men under battle conditions and with conspicuous courage.

Without hesitation I introduced myself and background. I then said, "Okay fellows, I hear you've got problems. No rank now, let's just talk about it and see what we can come up with." We did just that, with the chaplain joining in. They realized that they had compounded a bad situation when they dumped their duffle bags overboard. They were indeed contrite.

We finally decided the chaplain and I would go to the chief chaplain of the port. We would try and explain to him the background for the apparently defiant action. If we could win him over we might be able to get the ears of the Port Commanding Officer. Then we would hope for leniency and a new shipping date for the group.

That's just what happened. I did my damnedest as an advocate. My friend the chaplain backed me up every inch of the way. As subtly as I could, I worked in the idea of taking nurses from a number of units and grouping them all together. They could be placed in a section of a suitable boat. Unit identity was lost anyway. The colonel didn't respond much to that but I didn't expect him to. The look of thoughtfulness on his brow was enough.

The chaplain and I got a grudging concession that no charges would be brought, in return for model behavior. Mission accomplished we returned to camp and gave the word to our "clients." "Look guys, not one case of intoxication, not one fight, or some rank-happy clown will jump on you," I admonished.

It must have been about ten days later. The alert came for the group to which I was attached. We were to embark two mornings hence. The ship was the old transport the George Washington. Rather appropriate, I thought. At long last we made the truck ride to the swarming docks. The lines were long. Each man was checked twice against a list. The last check was at the foot of the gangplank. It seemed like the beginning of a rainbow.

I edged forward in line with my bulging bag. As I looked up at the ship I saw a GI trying to get my attention. It was the sergeant with the decorations and the combat medic emblem. He gave a wave and grinned as he edged along the ship's rail toward the upper end of the gangplank.

When I approached the foot of the gangplank I gave my name to the GI checking off the roster. He looked up suddenly and said, "Oh Major, there's something here for you. Looks like it's been following you around." The wrinkled envelope had scribbled notations on it but the Third Headquarters stamp on the upper left was legible.

The GI's pencil poised over the roster hesitatingly as if expecting some change in orders. Hastily, I tore open the envelope, read the two or three lines and broke into a chuckle.

"Everything okay Sir?" inquired the GI.

"Oh yeah. Just a thank you from my boss," I answered. Still chuckling, I shoved the piece of paper into my pocket adding to myself; "Both earthly and eternal." I picked up my bag and stepped on up the gangplank. I'd been a lieutenant colonel for about six weeks.

EPILOGUE

These heroes without guns brought home to their communities and families something more than most GI's. They had learned in the terribly realistic school of experience many of the things we take for granted in today's highly trained paramedics.

The infantryman put down his M1 rifle. The tank crew bade goodby to their armored steeds. Flight crews looked over their shoulders at aircraft they left at airbases and on carriers. Navy crews somewhat wistfully left their ships of war to be mothballed.

The enlisted medic brought home something different he need not forget. He could use it proudly when the occasion demanded.

In late July of 1956, I was driving from New London, New Hampshire to Meredith, New Hampshire to see one of my sisters. With me were two young daughters. About one-third of the way there I rounded a sharp curve and abruptly found myself looking at an overturned car. It had obviously just gone off the road. It was resting, not very steadily, on its right side. The two left wheels were still turning slowly.

Mine was the first car on the scene. I hit the brakes and pulled off the road. I got there in time to help the driver get his door open and inch him gradually out. He was only scratched and bruised with minimal bleeding. "Help my father," he said as he pointed to a large, fairly heavy man slumped down in the passenger's seat. Blood stained several places on his clothes. He was semi-conscious and moaning.

It was impossible to get the door open without righting the car. For that, we needed help. By this time other cars had stopped and about eight spectators were looking down at us from the roadside. I looked up and asked for some help from several men. No one made a move, although one man spoke up and said he wasn't going to take a chance on being sued. This was before the Good Samaritan law went into effect. The driver of the overturned car pleaded in vain. He had no takers.

We couldn't budge him without at least some uprighting of the car. In a couple of minutes another half-dozen men joined the spectators and I made another appeal for help. This time three youngish men in their thirties came bounding down the bank of the road.

"We have to get the car upright to get the door open enough to slide him out," I explained. "He's bleeding profusely too. Right arm, I think." We moved to the car to get it upright. At this point we were joined by two other men who had been watching. As the car came upright, two of the early volunteers moved to the passenger's door with me.

Even before the car was fully upright, we had the door three-quarters open.

"We'll get him out head first. Don't let his back buckle, could be a fracture," I warned. As we carefully and slowly extricated him from the car, I saw there was quite a lot of blood on his right arm. Before I could say a word, the fellow on that side removed the belt from his trousers and used it as a tourniquet on the man's upper arm.

My hand, under the injured man's back, was covered with blood. He was bleeding there as well. "Possible fracture left leg," murmured the other volunteer as the man's legs came out. He was unconscious now. We cut away his clothes to find a bleeding, but controllable, laceration on his back. "Let's get him in shock position," I said to the three. On a grassy spot we put his head about a foot lower than his feet.

I turned to the man that had been quick with the tourniquet and said, "You've done this before, haven't you?"

"Yeah," he replied. "Medic, Europe. First Army."

I turned my head to the other two, "Navy corpsman, South Pacific," one volunteered. The other man followed with, "Medic, Eighth Air Force. Europe."

"Congratulations, fellows. I was one too. Had a dental maxillo-facial team. Worked out of Third Army Headquarters."

I heard later the patient did pretty well. I checked.

As soon as I mention I was in Third Army, I hear the question. "What did you think of Patton?" It's a question I hear frequently, and I pause as a flood of memories and feelings sweep over me.

I never spoke with the General. I only saw him occasionally, but I felt his spirit and drive. It went down through the ranks. Perhaps my reaction to his death answers the question in a few words.

I was in Florida visiting my parents when General Patton was injured. His staff car was hit by a truck. From the nature of his injury, a broken neck, it seemed obvious he could not live. I thought I was prepared to accept his death. Yet when the news came over the radio that General Patton had died, much to my parents surprise and my own, I sat down in the nearest chair and cried.

Memories flashed across my mind bringing a ferment of emotion. Normandy. The French grandmother and her dying grandson. The wounded and the dying. Those I helped, those I couldn't help. The horror of the concentration camps, their smell — that awful, perverse act of chemistry. The confrontation with the German colonel in Apolda, and the sudden realization we were both human beings with but one Creator. The clash with the Russians in Strakonitz. And finally, that profound statement, "Unless we can talk to each other and become friends, it will be a rough few centuries."